I AM AN ALCOHOLIC

I AM AN ALCOHOLIC

BY

RAYMOND BLACKBURN

LONDON

ALLAN WINGATE

Published in 1959 *by*
ALLAN WINGATE (Publishers) Ltd
12 *Beauchamp Place, London, S.W.*3

Made and Printed in Great Britain
by the Ditchling Press, Ltd
Ditchling, Hassocks, Sussex

First impression March 1959

For
PAUL REAY

CONTENTS

Introduction

IT was the 8th October, 1945. I had recently been returned to Parliament as a Labour M.P. I was already known to a number of people partly because I had tabled an amendment with the support of nine other M.P.s to the resolution laid before the House of Commons pledging this country to support the United Nations. The amendment provided for Britain to insist on an effective international authority for the control of atomic energy. All day long I waited nervously to be called by the Speaker. Finally I heard him say, 'Captain Blackburn'. I was afire to speak and all my nervousness vanished as soon as I was on my feet and knew that I had the attention of the House. I said that throughout his entire history man had been engaged in war and had used the most effective weapons at his disposal; that for him to change now would be the most extraordinary reversal of character ever known; that we must decide on the minimum conditions necessary for the maintenance of peace and the enforcement of the rule of law and never compromise on any of the minimum conditions; that international control of atomic energy was such a minimum condition and could ensure that this discovery would be used for constructive purposes only and not for universal destruction. As I swept to my conclusion I quoted Whittier's hymn:

'O, brother man, fold to thy heart thy brother,
Where pity dwells the peace of God is there.
To worship rightly is to love each other.
Each smile a hymn, each kindly deed a prayer.'

When I resumed my seat Attlee, the Prime Minister, crossed the gangway to shake my hand in congratulation. Mr Churchill had listened intently and with evident approval.

It was, indeed, his support which I had always longed to enlist because he had been my hero from my schooldays onwards. He leaned forward to the Dispatch Box, looked across the floor of the House at me and wrote a note which he handed to the usher for transmission to me in full view of the House and crowded galleries. It was a supreme moment of triumph. I had sometimes dreamed that something like this could happen but never felt that there was even a remote possibility that my dream could come true.

I could hardly wait to hear the next speaker out before I rushed to the Strangers' Bar for several large gins. A friend of mine, a reporter, suggested that if I wished to continue drinking I should go elsewhere as reputations made over-night could be destroyed just as quickly. I took his tip and went out to a public house and then to the Gargoyle Club where I drank heavily into the early hours of the morning. A casual observer might have thought that I had some terrible burden of sorrow which I was drowning in drink. I ended up intoxicated—though not completely drunk. The next morning a terrible hangover affected my satisfaction at the friendly reports of my speech in the newspapers.

Why then did I want drink to be my familiar companion for ever at my elbow in success and failure, in prosperity and in poverty? Why, with a zest for life and wonderful oppor-tunities to pursue it, with a beautiful and loving wife and three healthy children, did I wish to follow the alcoholic path to self-destruction? Why did I insist on drinking life to the lees?

CHAPTER I

Early Days

LIKE a great many alcoholics I had a very strict upbringing. I was my father's favourite son, but that did not mitigate his anger when I did what was wrong—as happened very frequently. 'Fetch the wicket', he would say, and I would have to crawl under the stairs and bring a cricket-wicket to him with which he would hit me three times on the hand. If I flinched or made a fuss, the punishment would be more severe. My father was a great believer in the ethics of the Old Testament on which he had been brought up by his mother. He would often say to us, 'Spare the rod and spoil the child.' Although he did not teach us the theology of the Old Testament, he believed that on Sundays we should sit quietly or go for a walk after church and never be allowed to play. On weekdays, however, life was different and very interesting, for he loved to take me wherever he was going. As he was a Councillor as well as a doctor I saw a great deal of the world at an early age. I was in fact a precocious child.

Although born in Yorkshire of Yorkshire parents, I spent my early years in Bournemouth and, except for my visits to Poole with my father, in an ultra-respectable atmosphere.

When I used to go for walks with him, I noticed how respectful were the many men and women whom he knew. Their form of greeting was a grave raising of the hat. If they were his patients they were noticeably even more respectful than the others, hoping no doubt that they would not need his services but anxious to be on the best relations with him in case of emergency. A man's doctor is a highly important person in his life—particularly in Bournemouth where so many leisured people take an inordinate interest in the state of their health.

AX

He was largely a self-made man, the son of a wool-carder
of Cleckheaton in Yorkshire. He had been apprenticed to a
chemist but my grandfather had been thrown out of work
and unable to pay the balance of the fees. My father had
had to educate himself and pay his own way, had in consequence failed two years running for the degree of Member of
the Pharmaceutical Society and had with great difficulty
succeeded the third time. It was not until he was thirty-two
that he had been able to become a doctor. But by now almost
all trace of the homely Yorkshire brogue was gone except in
moments of severe crisis. His humble origin was a family
secret of which we were proud in private. He was M.D.
(*avec grand distinction* of Brussels), M.R.C.S., L.R.C.P. That
he was or ever had been M.P.S. was never mentioned.

Although choleric and strict, he had a strong sense of
humour. Like many people, he thought that, although this
was a powerful weapon when directed against others, it was
incapable of recoiling on himself. But I was not sure and
often pondered on the meaning of a cryptic remark he made
one day when we were out walking. I noticed that he had
failed for the third time to acknowledge the salute of a fine-
looking gentleman whom we had passed in the street. 'Is
there something wrong with that man, Daddy, that you
take no notice of him?' 'Certainly there is', my father
replied. 'Something very much wrong with him. I told him
three years ago that he would be dead within the year.'
But he did not laugh. So neither did I.

Largely due to intense personal tuition from my father
I won a top classical scholarship at Rugby school. He had
obtained all the examination papers for a dozen or more
years previously, with the result that in some subjects I was
likely to be set questions which I had had to answer over and
over again before. Moreover, the *viva voce* examination had
been rehearsed on countless occasions so that I could answer
quickly and decisively the questions usually put, such as
'What do you mean to be when you have left school?',
followed by the inevitable 'Why?'. My answers to these were:
'A barrister', and 'Because I like arguing', which in the
result set the Headmaster's Committee into a very good

humour with its obvious playful continuing gambit of
'What would you like to argue with me about?'. Little did
they know that the whole sequence had been carefully
rehearsed and the potential subjects for argument by me
with the Committee considered exhaustively.

So I landed in Tom Brown's house, the School House,
Rugby, a year younger than any boy in the school and very
much smaller, but with a high opinion of the capabilities of
the youthful Raymond Blackburn.

The steps which are taken by a public school to teach a
young man to conceal his conceit are painful. That I did not
find them more painful was largely due to my Spartan upbringing. The three smacks on the buttocks (protected only
by pyjamas) were hardly more unpleasant than the strokes
of the wicket which I had been wont to receive from my
father. I had already learned the wisdom of submitting with
as outwardly courageous a grace as possible to inevitable
punishment. The collective unpleasantness of my school
companions in reward for my bumptiousness and failure to
accept their conventions was far harder to bear. Adolescent
boys can be very cruel to one another. If I had not been
reasonably good at games I should have fared even worse.
Few boys at Rugby can have enjoyed their stay who did not
enjoy prowess at 'rugger' or cricket. But I thought—and
still think—it the best public school in the country.

Nevertheless the belief of the majority of people in the
great advantages of education at such establishments is
hardly justified. The main advantages are the diminishing
snob value and the acquisition of a certain accent and deport-
ment. The educational content itself is not remarkable.
I was a classical scholar and moved by slow stages to the
top classical form, the Upper Bench. In the Lower Bench
we had studied the *Oedipus Tyrannus* by Sophocles, until the
more zealous of my companions must have known every
line by heart. Some of them could even have translated it
direct into Latin verse. By some strange chance an examination paper at the end of term contained this question:
'Explain the *Oedipus Tyrannus* in terms of the general
purposes of Greek tragedy and with particular reference to

dramatic irony.' Because one day when very bored I had
read a book from the library, I knew the answer, but I was
the only boy in the class who did. Boys can and do spend
years on learning verbal gymnastics in dead languages
without understanding the philosophy of the great minds of
antiquity. That incredibly profound philosopher Heraclitus
is only a name in a poem famous for its translation by Cory.
His disciple Democritus, author of the atomic theory, is
unheard of. The beauties of Homer and the fire of Demos-
thenes are ignored by pedagogues who are blind to them (as
indeed happens very largely even with Shakespeare). It is
indeed part of the public school tradition to decry enthusiasm
in any form and to regard with suspicion excessive mental
energy that is not expended on dull well-worn subjects (where
the master knows or can find all the answers).

Perhaps the best side of public schools is their light-hearted
side—the absurd traditions, the eccentric master, the occasional humorist. In 1927, although 'lamb-singing' was
abolished—the requirement that new boys should sing a
song publicly—there was a mysterious ceremony called
'buck-jumping' in the School House. At the end of term the
junior members of the House knelt down in twos, opposite
one another, while those who had gained a distinction on the
rugger field jumped over them in stockinged feet. (Distinction at cricket did not qualify for being a 'buck'; far less any
other kind of distinction.) An even odder tradition required
that anyone entering a certain corridor should say aloud
'Up please' to placate the spirit of a 'fag' who was supposed
to have died on the spot in an accident when answering a
'fag call'. All prefects, namely those in the sixth form or
those specially given the same power (usually as a result of
excelling at games), had the right to two 'fags' or small boys
to clean their studies and make toast for them. They were
even entitled to call 'Fag!'—at which every fag had to run
as quickly as possible towards the caller, the last to arrive
being required to perform the duty required of him by the
prefect. This custom continued until I left and I once took
advantage of it for the entertainment of a visitor. The last
fag to arrive was let into the secret that it was a bogus call

and he was compensated by receiving a shilling instead of being required to do a 'fag'. The 'fagging' system was not entirely one-sided, as the fag-master was expected to make a small payment for the services—and if he were a decent boy, he would try to help his 'fag' if he got into serious trouble.

My main claim to fame was that in my last term I managed to secure the editorship of *The Rugbeian*. I had no literary background or pretensions and it was a strictly commercial adventure. I went round the Rugby shop-keepers, and by convincing them that I could treble the circulation, obtained a large number of advertisements. By enlisting the support of friends in various houses and offering them a small commission I was able to treble the circulation—*The Rugbeian* having the privilege that a boy could order it on his parents' account 'to go down on the bill'. As a result I was able to produce a much better school magazine and to pay contributors what they considered to be a substantial sum. I was leaving at the end of term, so I decided to appropriate the profits to certain purposes of my own. A few days before the end of term the Headmaster congratulated me on my success as Editor and then enquired to what school charity I would wish the profits to be devoted. I replied that, as a strong believer in private enterprise receiving its just reward, I had already dealt with this matter to my own satisfaction. He was furious, and while acknowledging that I was entitled to do what I liked, said that his view of my conduct would be reflected in his final report. Fortunately I was able to intercept this report and commit it to the drawing-room fire unread by anyone but myself, my father being then in New Zealand.

I was very glad to be able to leave school and anxious to get on with some practical job. My father wished me to go to Oxford, or Cambridge (where my brother was), but while he was in New Zealand I persuaded a solicitor in Bedford Row to take me on for a short trial period as a solicitor's clerk. By the time my father returned from New Zealand I had settled down and in his own words he was faced with a *fait accompli*. He paid the fee reluctantly for my articles.

These were in many ways the happiest years of my life. Yet I had no money (living on ten shillings per week) and often went without luncheon. I had no 'girl friend'. I went very rarely to the cinema, never to the theatre. My relaxations were playing 'rugger' on Saturday and going to the Temple Church to listen to their famous choir on Sunday. I acquired an almost passionate love for English Church music. The secret of my happiness was my absorption in my work. I appeared in Chambers before a High Court Judge before I was eighteen. I issued writs and summonses for judgment, drafted briefs, attended conferences with counsels, and, when I was not too busy, listened to the acknowledged masters of their profession pleading in Court. Lord Justice Scrutton, in spite of his squeaky voice, appeared to me to be the man closest on earth to the Almighty. I would rather have had one hour with him than with the King, the Prime Minister, Donald Bradman, or anyone else with the possible exception of Winston Churchill, whom I had been brought up to admire as a man whose courage and brilliance transcended the pettiness of politics

I believed passionately in the rightness of our client's cause —wherever there was any sort of case to be put up. If an action were compromised I was heartbroken. But my principal, a very able man devoid of ambition or interest in money, applied the brake of common sense to my enthusiasm and taught me many interesting facts about human nature which were almost beyond my comprehension. For instance, there was one case of about forty pounds' worth of Dutch bulbs supplied to a man in Covent Garden named Burnell, where he solved the mystery, like the proverbial armchair detective. The goods had been ordered from our clients, the importers of the Dutch bulbs, by telephone and confirmed by letter, headed 'Martin Burnell'. But he had not only failed to pay the bill: he had disappeared. I went round to Covent Garden and managed to meet a bookmaker called Walter Bond. He was a great character and pressed a cigar on me. We had two glasses of beer together—at that time two was my quota. He was fascinating in his reminiscences and eloquent on the astonishing disappearance of his former friend and customer Martin Burnell who, he said, was sure to turn up again soon. I took a great liking to him as a Dickensian character and described him in detail to my principal. He laughed till the tears ran down his cheeks and said, 'Why, you poor boob, it's obvious. Walter Bond is Martin Burnell, of course.'

But he was not quite right. Walter Bond, Bookmaker, was Walter Arthur Pleydell. I subpoenaed him under his correct name before Judge Sir Alfred Tobin and sought to prove that all three were one and the same man. Tobin (who defended Crippen in his youth) said: 'This is the most extraordinary case I have ever heard. The plaintiff subpoenaes a witness on his behalf and then alleges that witness to be really the defendant.' The judge appeared for a while to be on the defendant's side, but then said to Pleydell, 'If you know Burnell so well, I will give you a month to produce him', and added with a kindly smile at me, 'You know you should not quarrel with this young man.' Pleydell, not a whit abashed, replied, 'He and I are the best of friends, your Honour.'

Pleydell did not appear on the adjourned hearing, and judgment was given against him. But there was no happy ending. I met him and he offered me £20 in full settlement. He even offered me another £5 on the side—a huge sum to me in those days. 'If you don't take this, you will get nothing, not even your costs, and that is what most lawyers care about.' I refused. He said, 'Well, I took quite a fancy to you. So at least I shall see that you get some good advice. You are a very keen, quick-witted young man, but you talk too much. You should never show the world all the cards you keep up your sleeve.' Six weeks later he died of drink, or rather of a stroke brought on by his heavy drinking. The advice he gave me was good, but it would have been better if he had then warned me that the drink which was killing him might ruin me.

At that time, however, I had only just begun to drink and I would have taken no notice. Indeed, with my bowler hat, my stiff white collar, my umbrella and my ultra-correct manners, I seemed to many people to be a priggish young man. I had an occasional drink at my rugger club because it was the manly thing to do and enabled me to make friends with men I admired. But I disliked the taste of beer and at first even feared its effect. The first time I had a glass of beer I felt a little faint, although I managed to conceal the fact from my companions. I had had a horror of fainting from the day at school when I saw a boy faint. It took me weeks and even months to overcome my repugnance for the taste and effect of beer—but I was determined to show that I could drink as much as or more than the other members of the club with enjoyment and without ill-effects. By the time I was twenty-two I could drink a great deal without getting drunk—and what was worse, I was proud of it. I once drank nine pints of beer to the tune of 'Nine green bottles hanging on a wall'—and the interval between each pint was only enough to enable me to get my breath back. I was at least sensible enough not to drink large quantities of spirits for a bet. But that was because an Old Rugbeian had drunk a bottle of brandy for a bet on leaving school and had died immediately of heart failure.

Even so, it would be quite wrong to imply that my drinking habits in any way interfered with my life at his stage. I only once got drunk, and was terribly ashamed of it for months afterwards—going to ridiculous lengths to avoid people who knew about it. I had really done nothing more than get a little boisterous and noisy on Christmas Eve at lunchtime. But I had come back from the party to the office, and although most of the staff thoroughly enjoyed the fun, there was a certain lady who wanted to annoy my secretary and decided to complain. Fortunately my principal was out and the man in charge of the office was not only very decent and understanding but himself no mean performer with the bottle. 'Blackburn', he said, 'I am surprised at you. I have enjoyed getting into far worse states than you hundreds of times but I have had the sense so far to choose the time and occasion better. If I were you, I should go home'—and I did. At the time, of course, I did not believe that I was seriously under the influence of drink, let alone drunk, and if anyone had spoken to me more severely and less tactfully,

I should have retaliated and made the situation far worse. A long time elapsed before I risked making the same mistake again.

My hard work and interest in the law had its reward when I obtained the New Inn Prize and First Class Honours in the Solicitors Final, although I had had no oral tuition and had even managed to get a paid job before the completion of my articles. This job gave me an insight into the activities of some financiers and shook my faith in the unlimited virtues of free enterprise. I was engaged in civil actions arising out of the Pepper Case. It was a fascinating story, starting with a memorandum by a gentleman to the effect that the world's supply of pepper was 12,000 tons. Those engaged in the gamble to control the world's supply eventually bought more than the total of the world's estimated supply. There were two main explanations. In the first place a large number of Chinese peasants had stored pepper by way of accumulated wealth—much as French farmers are said to keep gold. This was presumably a tradition dating from hundreds of years ago when spices were the commodity so eagerly sought by Western adventurers, and the search for the quickest route to the spice islands led to many geographical discoveries. The second reason for the failure of the plan was even more startling. Pepper was dealt with—oddly enough—on the Metal Exchange. Brokers who were business rivals of those primarily engaged in the gamble sensed that something was wrong and that the financial resources of their opponents were limited, so they actually put on the market thousands of tons of nonexistent pepper. The bottom fell out of the market. The Banks closed down on their advances and the crash came. A former Tory Chancellor of the Exchequer had actually invested £50,000 of Bank money in the gamble. He was Reginald McKenna, Chairman of the Midland Bank. But, of course, he was not aware of all that was happening.

As nominee for my father, I spoke at the meeting of the Royal Mail Steam Packet Company when it went into liquidation, and although under twenty-one, I was elected the sole representative of the ordinary shareholders in the

liquidation. Here again I was astonished to find out how
great a gamble had gone on unknown to the shareholders,
and how great the sympathy was in many exalted quarters
for Lord Kylsant who was convicted, and for the partner in
Price Waterhouse and Company who was acquitted in the
criminal charges brought by Sir William Jowitt. When the
assets came to be realised I introduced a firm of stockbrokers
in the City to put up a bid in opposition to the bid which
Sir William McLintock as Liquidator was proposing to
accept from another firm of stockbrokers. The two firms did
some kind of a deal and in the result, as I discovered by
accident, a proportion of the shares of Royal Mail Realisa-
tion were sold to a company controlled by Lord Kylsant's
brother, Lord St Davids. This was the extraordinary result
of my intervention. But, of course, there was nothing sinister
about it. When very large sums of money are involved there
is little real competition because there are only a few firms
or companies with the necessary money who are interested
in the particular kind of business concerned.

In 1938 I went to New Zealand on family business and
travelling back across the Pacific and the U.S.A. went round
the world. It was a very different world then from now. Much
of the glory and prestige of the British Empire still survived.
On this voyage so much of my strict Victorian upbringing
remained with me that, although I stayed a month in San
Francisco and had quite enough money with me to enjoy
myself thoroughly, I never even kissed a girl. I was obsessed
with the idea that as an Englishman I must show myself to
be somehow different from the 'lesser breeds without the
law'. The only relaxation which seemed to me to be permitted
was drink, and at this time I had an extraordinary capacity
for a young man—as is common with alcoholics. I began to
acquire the cocktail habit and to feel the need for a drink at
six o'clock. But I still had not the faintest idea of the insidious
danger to me of such habits.

On my return to England I proposed unsuccessfully some
forty times to a beautiful girl from New Zealand and
eventually persuaded her to marry me. There are some

subjects over which even in this exhibitionist age the veil of secrecy should be drawn, and this is surely one of them. My marriage was happy for very many years and when it finally broke up—as I now see it—the fault was mine. As, however, the main object of this book is to write about alcoholism from the point of view of a self-confessed alcoholic, a word should be said about my wife's attitude to drink. She constantly tried to discourage me from drinking to excess. What neither she nor anyone else realised until it was too late is that it was not possible for me as an alcoholic to moderate my drinking. My only salvation lay in total abstinence. But, of course, at this stage and indeed until long after the war was ended, no one could have brought me to believe that I was even a potential alcoholic.

Those years before the war seem now to belong to a different age. To me the British Empire appeared greater and more secure than ever in its history. Neither Nazism nor Communism seemed strong enough to have any chance of overthrowing it. Even if war came with Germany—as by 1939 I believed probable—the idea that France might collapse never occurred to me as a serious possibility. By comparison with pre-war years, the Englishman of today, in spite of the Welfare State, seems infinitely less sure of himself, and the world outside Britain far more hostile and dangerous. But the relative security of the pre-war years carried with it many disadvantages from the point of view of a young man. In Tory Britain it seemed very difficult for a young, ambitious man to get on in the world unless he had great wealth or high connections. When once I remarked to Mr Churchill that he was born with a golden spoon in his mouth, Mrs Churchill said: 'No more of a golden spoon than any other younger son of the younger son of a Duke!' Such an entrée to life was invaluable in the years before the war.

The life of a London solicitor seemed very tame to me. I was still fascinated by the law, but I was really on the wrong side of my profession. My talents were for advocacy rather than for the routine work of a lawyer's office. I should have been a barrister rather than a solicitor—as most of my legal colleagues told me. I intended to read for the Bar but the

war interfered with my plans. Strangely enough, the outbreak of war greatly excited and secretly delighted me. I had
longed for something interesting to happen which would
break the monotony of my life. Above all, I had often dreamed
that I would return to a grateful country as a war hero
covered with ribbons and glory. So I lost no time in getting
into the army.

CHAPTER II

The War

WITHIN a week or two of the outbreak of war I went to Sandhurst. As a private soldier drawing marriage allowance I received seven shillings a week and my wife received twenty-four shillings a week. Four shillings a week was deducted from my pay for various extras, so that every Friday I saluted and said, 'Thank you, sir', for three shillings which I immediately gave to my batman. At Sandhurst we drilled and sat in civilian clothes for the first six weeks as there were not enough uniforms to spare for us. It seemed and still seems to me that far too much time was taken in trying to turn us out as first-class soldiers and practically no time in teaching us to be officers. Drill, turn-out and what is termed 'bull' were all-important. Nevertheless there were a few lessons which were later to be found useful, notably the sequence of orders: information, intention, method, administration and intercommunication. There is no doubt that an orderly habit of mind is invaluable in emergencies. Later I found few officers who stuck to the simple rules, and their orders suffered greatly as a result. Of course, a great man can afford to break the rules, but very few of us are great. In any event, the best and most experienced officers of all observed the rules, as I was later to discover.

A fortnight after arrival I stopped the General on the front square when he was off duty and tried respectfully to make the point that we should receive tactical training. Although he was polite, he passed on the fact to my Company Commander, who finally recommended that I was unfit to be an officer—by which he really meant that I was unfit to be a private soldier. The sole ground of my unfitness alleged

by him, was my lack of a sense of discipline. The new
Commandant, Brigadier Kemp-Welch, sent my Company
Commander out of the room and said, 'I would never plough
the man who scored that try on Saturday.' (I played rugger,
hockey and soccer for the company.) 'But for God's sake
don't talk so much.' Walter Arthur Pleydell alias Walter
Bond alias Martin Burnell had told me the same thing seven
years before. The Brigadier told my Company Commander
to make me Intelligence Officer on the next exercise. It was
a pitch-black night and I had to lead the company through
a thick wood over the moor to its position for a night attack.
Half way during the journey my Company Commander
said, 'You've lost your way, but I don't blame you. Even I
don't know it.'

'I have not', I replied, and I led the company straight to
its immediate objective. He had the grace to tell the story to
the assembled company the next day, but I half suspect that
he thought it was luck. It was not. My friends for the
night had spent hours over the ground and I could almost
have found my way through that wood blindfold.

I must admit that my Company Commander had a point
in ascribing to me a lack of a sense of discipline. But for the
kindness of R.S.M. Brand I might have been in serious
trouble. I was on sentry duty on a bitterly cold night at the
gates. He was walking home and I pulled a half-bottle of
rum out of my greatcoat and offered him a swig. He was
obviously horrified by the gesture, but kindly explained to
me the serious nature of the offence and then said nothing
more about it.

The hours of work were very long and the drill and P.T.
very tiring. My two best friends were John Aldworth, afterwards killed on D-Day leading his company of the Royal
Ulster Rifles, and J. M. Crook, afterwards 'ploughed' and
returned to civilian life, but later engaged as a glider pilot
in Sicily and wounded at Arnhem. The three of us used to
take it in turns at the early morning parade, when it was
still dark, to answer the names of the other two. We were
never caught, but again it would have justified the complaint
of lack of discipline if we had been. Later I was to discover

officers in very important positions committing similar
offences, which if discovered might have ruined them. The
great offence in the Army is to be caught.

I asked to be posted to the East Yorkshire Regiment—the
XVth of Foot—and I was duly posted to Beverley. There I
found the life of a junior second lieutenant far more miserable
than that of an officer cadet at Sandhurst. But senior officers,
who are kept hanging about regimental depots, are rarely in
a good mood and generally those in entrenched positions
there are unlikely to be good regimental officers or they
would be commanding battalions on training or in the field.
The East Yorkshire Regiment has a fine reputation and as
soon as I had left the depot I had a wonderful time wherever
I went. I am therefore reluctant to record that conditions
for both officers and private soldiers were very unhappy and
not improved by a major who had never seen active service
but considered himself as a regular, entitled to be appallingly
rude even to volunteer officers with 1914-1918 ribbons on
their tunics. There was a minority of disgruntled regular
officers, who seemed even to have sadistic tendencies. Later,
when posted to a regular battalion, I found the regular
officers there not only gentlemen in the best sense of the
word but far less conscious of their rank than territorial
officers in a territorial battalion.

To go to France in early 1940, as I did, was a great
experience. En route for our 4th Battalion, I stayed at a
camp near the lovely city of Rouen and then went by slow
and somewhat uncomfortable stages to the area where the
B.E.F. was stationed in readiness for an attack, which was
not really expected. When we had to stop at little villages on
the way, we were more than once fêted by the local mayor.
Toasts were drunk to the Entente Cordiale and very pretty
speeches made in a *patois* which I found difficult to follow.
But the friendliness and generosity of many French people in
the north of France are a most pleasant memory. Moreover,
the poorer the district the warmer the welcome.

On May 10th, 1940, I was a Second Lieutenant in the 2nd
Battalion (a regular Battalion) of the East Yorkshire
Regiment at a village near Lille, close to the Belgian border.

The Division was commanded by Major-General B. L.
Montgomery, then ranking low in the military hierarchy
but greatly admired by the most efficient officers of the
B.E.F., including himself. As Commander of the 9th Infantry
Brigade he had been wont to say, 'When I am Commander
of the 3rd Division, this is the way I will do it.' It was
certainly a good division, comprising the 7th Guards Brigade
(two regular Coldstream and one Grenadier Battalion), our
Brigade the 8th (two regular line battalions and one territorial) and the 9th Brigade of three regular battalions.
General Montgomery was already beginning to emphasise
the vital importance of training on Divisional exercises in the
field. At first, however, I was inclined to dismiss him in my
mind as rather a Blimp because one day when visiting our
Company he said to my Company Commander, 'What school
did your new subaltern go to?' The answer 'Rugby' being
given, he said, 'Then you've got the best of the bunch.' The
question, 'What school were you at?' was the first I was
asked on many occasions (particularly by my Company
Commander at Sandhurst). It still seems to me very wrong,
although I personally was to find ex-public schoolboys
generally made excellent officers. Strangely enough, Ernest
Bevin was to acknowledge this, but with the wrong illustration. 'When they talk of Eton and 'Arrow, I remember we
were thankful enough for their boys in the Battle of Britain.'
Actually a very high proportion of the Battle of Britain
pilots were secondary-school boys. Etonians and Harrovians
abounded in the Guards rather than the R.A.F.

When the real war started, our journey up to the front
line in Belgium was like Ferdinand the Bull's triumphant
progress to Madrid. The flags were flying and the pretty
girls cheered us and threw flowers into the lorries. They
seemed to think victory was round the corner. Most of us
were wondering whether it would be like 1914 all over again,
but probably not quite so bad. None of us would have thought
it possible that within six weeks Paris would have fallen.

It seems certain that some sense must have warned me of
the danger of alcohol, because I decided to have nothing to
drink during the campaign. Just before the real war started

I had been in a colossal party with an officer senior to myself as a result of which he was placed under arrest for being drunk. The army tradition is that the senior officer takes the blame for the others. I did my best to persuade my friend that he could not be convicted and should not accept a reprimand from the General, but he was so keen to take part in the battle that he disregarded my advice. The charges could never have been sustained as all the witnesses against him were French civilians now separated from us by the tide of the war. This incident made me determined to remain strictly teetotal, and so I did, to the surprise of my brother officers, until I ceased to be in command of my men on arrival at the beach at La Panne.

Battle was first joined between the German Army and the British at Louvain where the two other Brigades of our Division held the canal, our Brigade being in reserve. My battalion marched many weary miles to reach a village behind the front line, but it was thrilling to hear the rumble of the guns. I kept thinking of the first lines of *Mort d'Arthur*, 'So all day long the noise of battle rolled.' Our own twenty-five pounders from the field in which my platoon was entrenched made a colossal noise throughout the next two or three nights. They were giving support to the Grenadiers and the Royal Ulster Rifles on the canal, but ominously the enemy gunfire seemed to shift from the front ahead of us round our flank. I could not believe that there had been a break-through in Louvain; nor was there, but the success of the German army elsewhere necessitated the orders for withdrawal that came up. For a few hours we were the rearguard, after the withdrawal of the brigades who had been in Louvain, but to my disappointment, I saw no sign of a German. In general, throughout the campaign on the sector of the hard core of the B.E.F. (the 1st, 2nd, 3rd and 4th Divisions) which constituted most of the regular army in France and Belgium in the month of May, 1940, there was not only no loss of ground as a result of enemy attack, but when we withdrew, the enemy did not follow on our heels.

From Louvain, after holding for a few hours an intermediate position, we marched back to Brussels which had been declared an open city. The Belgians were as friendly as ever, but tears were in the eyes of many as they tried to be cheerful. None said '*adieu*'—many '*au revoir*'. The troops were kept in a square all day—but I managed with another officer to go into a restaurant. The owner offered us all he had and would take no payment. He told us we would be back eventually, but how long it would take he hated to think. This was the spirit of the Belgian people as a whole.

We then held a succession of positions on the banks of canals. The exact posts which the sections of my platoon were to occupy were already selected in advance. Two sections were in slit trenches, two or three yards from the edge of the canal and about fifty yards distant from one another. The third section was in reserve, with platoon headquarters between fifty and a hundred yards to the rear. Some concealment was possible for the reserve section—none for the forward sections. The armament of each platoon apart from rifles consisted of three light machine-guns, an anti-tank rifle (.55) and a two-inch mortar. My two-inch mortar was without a firing pin and therefore useless; it was not my fault as the need for a replacement had been reported many times; supplies of such spare parts were almost non-existent even for a crack regular division. Ammunition for the anti-tank rifle was so scarce that the soldier who eventually fired it had only fired five practice rounds, and when I fired it to replace him, against an armoured car, it was the first time I had done so and I was more frightened of the recoil than of the enemy.

There is no doubt that the tactics employed over the disposition of our troops in defence of the canals were mis-taken. Not long after our return a directive was issued, which must have emanated from 'Monty', to the effect that con-cealment should be treated as at least as important as field of fire. The correct way to hold these canals was to cover them from well-concealed positions by day and patrol them by night. The effect of holding the canal banks in the way we did was to offer easy targets to the enemy mortars which probably accounted for more of our casualties than all other enemy weapons combined. The casualties would have been even heavier if the troops had not been well trained in digging narrow and deep slit trenches which provided good cover even from mortars.

The positions which we held were very strong indeed. Not once did my platoon look in serious danger of losing ground. For example, we took over from a company of the Coldstream Guards a position on a canal after our withdrawal from Alost. For some reason which I could not understand there was no officer and the sergeant-major of the Coldstream's painted a gloomy picture of the situation. (There was no take-over by platoons as is usual.) But when I got to the canal, I found the following picture. There was a bridge over the canal on which were two machine-guns manned by the Middlesex Regiment. To the left of the bridge was a large open field, and at the back of the field a large barn. My job was to hold the canal for an area of about four hundred yards. To my left were a company of the 4th Battalion Royal Berkshire Regiment—the territorial unit of our brigade. Only one hundred and twenty men of this battalion returned to Britain, the remainder being casualties from mortars, and from a disastrous counter-attack about which I shall write later. They lost very heavily at this position from mortaring.

My platoon headquarters and reserve section were in front of the barn. The canal was wide, and although there were a few trees on the other side, the field of fire was good. The right-hand section contained the anti-tank rifle with Nixon, the only man who had fired it. The road leading to the bridge on the other side of the canal was well covered. For thirty-six hours there was no attack, although according to the Coldstreams there had been several attacks on the two days before our arrival. Then at dawn two or three vehicles which I wrongly thought to be light tanks, but must have been armoured cars, came up the road. Our section posts were fired on with tracer shells about six inches long, one of which split open the head of a man in the left-hand section. (He was the only man killed in my platoon during the entire campaign.) We fired back from the right-hand

section with the anti-tank rifle. The light machine-gunner in
the left-hand section fired also, although I did not then
realise it. So did the machine-gunners on the bridge. After
about a quarter of an hour the firing ceased, two of the
armoured cars remaining on the road, having been put out
of action. One hour afterwards, the mortaring started—to
which no retaliatory action could be taken. This caused the
very severe casualties among the Berkshires on our left. My
own men squatted at the bottom of the deep slit trenches,
with their heads three feet below ground. One man would
occasionally pop up his head to see whether there was any
sign of the enemy. But, of course, there was not. For them to
have attacked us in such a strong position would have been
suicidal. They would not even have reached the edge of the
canal.

At night I used to prowl at the other side of the canal with
a soldier in my platoon named Greene. We crossed the canal
by using a sort of punt. We could never find any Germans,
although they were undoubtedly in a village about a mile
away, which was too far away for us to investigate. I mention
this because of an extraordinary incident that occurred on
the last day. All was quiet and there was nothing and no one
to see on the deserted countryside ahead of us except for the
armoured cars (now suddenly burning for some strange
reason) and the grotesquely swollen bellies of the cows that
had been shot either by accident or by way of target practice.
Suddenly to my intense astonishment came orders to with-
draw at nine o'clock that night. An Artillery officer came to
us and explained that his Regiment was heavy artillery and
he had been ordered to use up all his remaining ammunition.
Our Colonel had sent him to me to tell him on what targets
it should be used. It was little enough use, but I directed it
into what I believed to the enemy headquarters in the
village.

I was sick at heart to leave so good a position, and so
were the men. But I failed to keep an eye on Greene. He
managed to slip away and find a bottle of brandy in a
chateau. By seven o'clock he was roaring drunk in the left-
hand forward section position and exhorting his comrades

not to be ——— cowards like the ——— officers and run
away. He would fight it out alone if need be and beat the
whole ——— German Army on his own. I went up there and
tried to reason with him, but it was hopeless. We had to go
in a few minutes and he might prejudice the other men's
lives. He jumped out of the trench—a very stupid act in
daytime. I pulled out my pistol and supported by two other
men said, 'I order you escorted by these two men back to
company headquarters. Drop your rifle or I will shoot you.'
His answer was to swing his rifle at me. I dodged—almost
ran away from him. One of the other men caught him a
blow with a rifle and he was carried away. Afterwards we
became the firmest of friends again; it is impossible to
harbour grievances for long in such conditions, and after four
more days I persuaded the authorities to drop any charges
against him. Sober, he was a wonderful soldier—a brave
man who would volunteer for anything and then not take an
unnecessary risk. Like many other brave men, he was later
killed in training in England.

From that position we went to Wattrelos, where we were
not much troubled by the enemy. An extraordinary conversation took place in the officers' mess about death. The news
had come through unofficially that we were in very serious
trouble. Our acting Company Commander—a regular
officer—was a very decent fellow and was about to take over
the job of Intelligence Officer, as the normal Intelligence
Officer had been wounded and our own Company Commander was returning to duty from elsewhere. There was therefore no particular reason why he should be in even as great
danger as the rest of us, particularly as our Colonel did not
expect the Intelligence Officer to take the same risks as
himself. Moreover, although I did not hold it against him,
he had not once visited the forward platoon positions and
seemed to have a salutary regard for his own skin. I am not
implying that he was a coward or that he would not have
done his duty in any circumstances, but he was the reverse
of a 'death or glory' soldier. He had been very depressed
after we left Brussels, in which there lived a girl with whom
he was in love. Suddenly after dinner at Wattrelos he said

that he was quite certain that he would be killed within the next fortnight. Nothing we said could show him the absurdity of so confident a prediction. I laughed at it, but when he was gone, 'R' and 'O', two brother officers, said they were convinced he was right. That evening was the last time I saw him—but on the frequent occasions on which the Colonel visited the front line, the Intelligence Officer was not with him. I felt sure that the prediction would prove wrong. But he was hit most unluckily by a stray shell on the beach and died instantly. Perhaps if he had courted more the danger about which he had a premonition, he would have survived. He said he hated the idea of death, but I do not believe he was afraid and he certainly did everything which duty demanded, calmly and well. This is the only incident I have known which appeared to justify the time theories of J. W. Dunne which J. B. Priestley has popularised. It is well known in the Regiment.

At Wattrelos the brigade was ordered to counter-attack. There was no conceivable purpose for the counter-attack other than allegedly to restore morale. But the morale did not need restoring, and if anything had been able to shake it, such a counter-attack would have been the very thing to do so. The 4th Royal Berks. were ordered to counter-attack across open ground. The enemy positions were not known and the artillery support was very slight. The men were mown down, but the objectives were reached and about six Germans taken prisoner. The German machine-gunners who had done the damage quietly disappeared.

Our battalion was luckier, being ordered to attack through the town. I issued the correct orders to my platoon, and then told them that as the real purpose of the attack was to restore morale and I knew there was nothing wrong with the morale, I did not propose to take the orders too seriously. Two very experienced regular soldiers volunteered to act as scouts. We skirted round the backs of houses and once had to run from cover to cover up a main street. But the Germans on this side of the town ran away, as they saw no good targets and did not want to be encircled. If any man had been hit, I would certainly not have risked losing any more

lives. As we were only supposed to stay on our objective for
half an hour, it made no difference what we did—and I
should certainly have made a mistake in map-reading and
said that we had already reached our objective. As it was,
mainly owing to the skill of the two soldiers I have described,
we did reach our objective. This time, however, instead of
going ahead with a futile and highly dangerous reconnais-
sance, I entered a house with a few men, searched in vain
for food and, finding none, played on the piano the only two
pieces which I knew—*Jesu, Joy of Man's Desiring* (Bach) and
Beethoven's *Minuet in G*. This oddly enough gave me a
reputation for cool courage—when really it proved nothing
of the sort!

From Wattrelos we went back to an intermediate position
before taking up our final stand on the line Furnes—
Nieuport. At this position, although we could hear some
firing, we were given to understand there was no
danger of a serious attack for twenty-four hours. Suddenly
the order came up that everyone must be on some troop-
carrying vehicles within half an hour or they would be left
behind. It was the only time we ever received snap orders or
withdrew suddenly under enemy pressure. The troops were,
of course, quite unprepared to leave so quickly, as although
a few stray bullets were whizzing in the air there was no sign
of a serious attack. They grumbled and were so slow in
obeying my orders that I was terrified that we should miss
the trucks and be left behind. My responsibility in that event
would have been grave. In my agitation I shouted out
'Quick, you bastards!' over and over again and that moved
them all right, but they looked as if they would have gladly
killed me. There is one name by which a Yorkshireman or a
'Geordie' should never be addressed and that is 'bastard'. In
the South the word does not carry so ill a meaning: I have
even heard it used in a certain context as a sign of admiration
for some tough and ruthless action which was however felt
to be justified. Not so in the North. Even in the dire perils
of the next few days I could tell that the words rankled and
that no explanation could justify their use. As it was, we
only just reached the trucks in time. There was heavy

shelling on the road seven or eight miles away. We stopped the trucks and crouched in the ditch. Even then some were hit. I received a blow in the small of the back, but it was only a ricochet.

CHAPTER III

Dunkirk and After

IT was dark by the time we reached Furnes, some of which was blazing. It was here that during the next few days the Guards held up the German attack. Our brigade—the 8th Infantry Brigade—were to the north of Furnes on the Nieuport-Furnes canal. My own company was assigned to cover the canal in front of the village of Wulpen. About four o'clock in the morning we trudged wearily up the road leading to the bridge over the canal in front of Wulpen. (Napoleon, when asked what was the finest form of courage, replied: 'Four o'clock in the morning courage.') To my surprise there was a figure sitting in the driver's seat of a staff car about one hundred yards short of the canal. I went up to him and, as he appeared to be asleep, placed my hand on his shoulder. The body slumped forward and I saw the bullet-hole in the windscreen.

'Willie' Spencer, our Company Commander, asked me to explore the ground to the right so that we could find our exact positions. This took some time and it was about nine o'clock in the morning before we had finally taken over from the company which we relieved. Spencer ordered the Company Quartermaster Sergeant, whose nickname was 'Biff', to serve tea. Biff, like the rations, was exhausted and said he literally could not move. I poured a whole jug of cold water over him, to the intense enjoyment of those present. He gave me a very ugly look and said, 'I will not forget this', but he proceeded to get the tea served.

The next-door platoon sergeant (a man named Fenwick) and I explored two or three boats or barges on the canal at night in the hope of finding food. Our only finds were two tins of sardines and a dead man. I have since often wondered

B

how many times old scores were paid off with impunity in areas near the battle zone.

The following night we were moved back to the area of the canal close to the bridge. The eerie figure of the driver was still slumped at the wheel and bullets occasionally whistled by him. My platoon was forward on the bridge—the foremost section actually on the canal itself. There were a few buildings nearby, and I managed to get my first real sleep since May 10th in the basement of one of them. I had given orders to be awakened after three hours, but they were countermanded by Willie Spencer who arrived during the night to have a look round. The following morning there was heavy mortaring and a certain amount of shelling. I went back to company headquarters to see Spencer. The cellar of his farmhouse was full of wounded men—some groaning. I noticed a red stain on Spencer's side, and when we looked to see the cause, we found that he had been wounded. For over an hour since being hit he had not realised that he was wounded. The same thing had happened to my batsman earlier. Few wounds seem to cause immediate pain, as the shock causes numbness. Spencer had to be taken away as his leg was stiffening.

The next few days until our final withdrawal were uncomfortable, but by no means unbearable. There was mortaring and sniping and an occasional burst of machine-gun fire if anyone appeared to move in daylight. But our defensive position on the canal was a strong one and it would have needed a very determined attack after careful preparation to have any chance of dislodging us. There were constant rumours that the Germans had crossed the canal either to the right or to the left of us. I do not believe there was any truth in these rumours, but they could have been damaging to the morale of men who had had practically no food and little sleep for days. There appears to me to be a tremendous natural tendency to over-estimate the strength of one's enemy in battle. The accurate assessment of one's opponent is of crucial importance and it is scarcely less dangerous to overestimate than to underestimate him. Towards the end of May 1940 it is very unlikely that the Germans could

have mounted an attack in this area strong enough to effect
serious penetration of our defences, which were on a narrow
front. The supreme danger was that boldness on the part of
the enemy combined with weak resistance on our part might
have given him a victory to which his actual strength on the
ground did not entitle him. This must have happened elsewhere, but it certainly did not happen between Furnes and
Nieuport. However, the achievement of holding the line—
indeed, the whole so-called 'miracle of Dunkirk'—has been
grossly exaggerated. Nothing that I saw at any time made
me change my first opinion that we could have held this
line indefinitely.

The morale of the troops was all-important. The officer in
the neighbouring platoon had been withdrawn and I was
the only officer in the company who was forward of company
headquarters. It was reported to me that a section post of
this platoon had received a direct hit by a mortar. One of
the men named Taverner had a serious compound fracture of
the leg and was in great pain. I visited the section and
decided that the only thing to do was to try to get him out
immediately—although the strict orders were that there was
to be no movement in daylight. Taverner's continued
presence in the section post was most inadvisable—quite
apart from the fact that he could not have been evacuated
to England, if he had not been got back quickly to the
beach. There were no stretchers or stretcher bearers.

I tried to run him on my back, but when I had to rest, he
begged me to shoot him on the spot, so great was his pain.
I have since been told that had I continued to run him on
my back for the three hundred yards to the farmhouse, he
might well have died from the shock.

I went back to the section post, leaving Taverner in the
open. A man named Cairns agreed to try to help me to get
him to company headquarters. We went back to the farmhouse and hacked down a door to serve as a stretcher on
which we got Taverner back to the farmhouse. I was at the
time convinced that the Germans refrained from firing at us
because they knew we were carrying back a wounded man.
Taverner was put on a carrier and got back to Britain,

although the leg had to be amputated. This whole incident surely proves that officers should have a special issue of some pain-killing drug for use in action in circumstances such as these. It is typical of the Army that young men can be trusted with the lives of men in action but not with small sums of money or with drugs. The loss of a pair of boots is an enormous matter requiring the detailed attention of three officers or a court of enquiry. The loss of men in battle sometimes seems to be an affair of much less importance. Men will give their lives but not their money for their country, and the country seems itself to adopt much the same attitude.

The night we left the canal the Colonel came up to visit us. He was obviously very tired but he still looked very much alive. All was quiet on the front. He asked me the way to the company on our right as he had not the time to go back to battalion headquarters and up again. He had to strike across country some five hundred yards to the rear of the canal. I told him that I had better accompany him—to which he reluctantly agreed. As we came to a track in the rear of our position heavy shelling from our own artillery opened up on us. I did not feel that it was a satisfactory idea to be wounded or killed by our own gunners. I jumped into a hollow by the side of the track. The Colonel turned to me in amazement, saying, 'What on earth are you doing down there?' I had no alternative but to carry on. Fortunately our artillery was short of ammunition and the shelling ceased before long.

We started thinning out at about dusk. As the officer, I was the last man on the canal and as I peered across it for the last time, I could see no sign of activity at all. Absolute silence reigned. It seemed absurd for us to be withdrawing.

I got my platoon into a lorry. The driver turned right at a cross-roads and if I had not stopped him we would have been driven straight into the arms of the Germans at Nieuport. It was a great relief to arrive at the beach where according to the orders we had received, military rank was at an end and we were to split up and follow the principle of 'sauve qui peut'. I told those members of my platoon who wanted to stay with me that it was to their advantage and mine to say goodbye and meet again on the other side. I did in fact see a squad of Guardsmen marching very smartly on the beach—but it was not a sensible thing to do as the beach was constantly being 'strafed' by low-flying fighters. We tried to shoot them down with rifles—there were plenty to be picked up on the beach. But I thought that it was a very forlorn hope as the pilots must have had bullet-proof protection.

The sight of men standing up to their knees in water waiting for boats for hour after hour was most depressing. 'Frightfully *infra dig.*, what?' said a young regular subaltern standing behind me. I admired the calm manner in which a naval officer, who cannot have long left school, prevented his boat from being overloaded. 'There's no need for worry, chaps. We'll get you all off before long.' I decided to look for some food in the houses near the beach which were, of course, deserted. But I had no luck.

Coming out of one of them I saw Biff, the Company Quarter-Master Sergeant, and asked him if he had yet for-given me for pouring the cold water over him. The incident still rankled, but we sang together our favourite song, 'Mine eyes are dim, I cannot see; I have not brought my "specs" with me.' But my eyes were not so dim that they did not notice a keg of ration rum which I immediately requisitioned. For the first time during the campaign I broke my decision not to drink and on this occasion and this alone I proved right. We had a very good party to which we invited a number of our colleagues. Later an irate Guards' Colonel came up to me and protested at my having made use of some of the Guards' issue of rum. However, there was nothing he could do about it. By this time I was naturally popular with a number of chaps who then proceeded to find an old boat and drag it to the sea. We rowed out to a ship which had seen service in World War One, a major in my Regiment trying to regulate the strokes of the oars with the words 'In, out. In, out', and with the air of a cox at Henley. I had to cling to the ship to keep the boat next to it as the men clambered out. We had a lot of difficulty over the last two men, one of whom was wounded. At the critical moment the ship was hit by a bomb and I had to take a split-second decision whether to get on the ship or stay with the wounded man and his comrade. I got on the ship and have regretted it ever since.

The ship was packed with soldiers, who raised their rifles when a fighter-bomber attacked the ship which was obviously in poor shape. At the last second the fighter-bomber swung away and we breathed a sigh of relief. 'Well, we're all right now', I said to the naval officer standing near me who had been exhorting us not to move about. 'Don't you be too sure about that', he replied. 'She's very groggy and she still might sink.' Never has Dover looked so beautiful as on that day.

Our battalion—indeed the whole Division—was completely re-equipped before June 16th, the day Paris fell, when we were inspected by the King, looking excellently cool and confident. One battalion, the 4th Royal Berks., came back with only 120 men. Its command had been given to a company commander in our battalion who was wearing the badges of a lieutenant-colonel. General Montgomery, the Divisional Commander, asked him to report whether his unit was fit to go into battle again with the reinforcements he had received. The lieutenant-colonel said that he greatly regretted that he could not report his battalion fit for battle. He added, 'It has been a great honour to serve in your division, sir, and I regret having to leave it.' 'You need not worry about that', said 'Monty', 'I would not dream of letting so valuable an officer leave my division.' So that day the lieutenant-colonel became a major again, and was assigned to command headquarters company. Nearly two years elapsed before he got a command again.

During that unforgettable summer of 1940, our division moved from Frome in Somerset to Sussex, and was then withdrawn on the express instructions of the Prime Minister into general reserve in the neighbourhood of Cheltenham. At first we practised assaults on hills which resembled cliffs. I was very puzzled by this as it seemed inconceivable that we were going to invade Europe. There was, however, a secret plan to recapture the Channel Islands. The morale of the troops was very high. One of my corporals said to me conversationally one day, 'You know, sir, the war will be all

over by this time next year.' I could not understand what
on earth he meant and said so. 'Ah', he said, with a superior
air, 'we shall invade France before the summer is out and
this time we will push them right back into Germany.' It
seems incredible, but this man, who was in other respects
quite intelligent, really believed what he was saying.

The Colonel had made me Intelligence Officer, and I so
rarely left his side that our inseparability became a joke at
Brigade Headquarters. He had been given the D.S.O. for his
services in May and the sergeant of the platoon next to me
had received the M.M. I made him my Intelligence Sergeant,
but by October he had been commissioned in another
Regiment and in November I received a letter from Major
Fenwick, M.M. The reputation of the 3rd Division stood
very high, particularly as its commander, General Montgomery, was clearly marking himself out for high command.
As soon as we had regrouped at Frome he gave one of his
lectures to all officers on the recent campaign. It was the
first time many of us had heard him and we were astonished
at his eloquence—a quality hardly to be expected of a soldier.
Simplicity, self-assurance, clarity, determination and a dry
humour produced a fascinating if not altogether attractive
combination. Few men have been great speakers without
being great egotists. 'Monty' may well have stressed his ego
as part of a deliberate policy on his part. When I stayed at his
headquarters after the war was over, I suggested this to
him as tactfully as I could, and he replied that supreme
confidence in their commander makes a vital contribution to
the spirit of troops and that men tend to take you at your own
valuation. The frequent attacks on 'Monty' by officers of
the old school ignored the fact that most people suffered
intense boredom in the army, from which 'Monty's' tricks
and mannerisms of all kinds were a relief. His great merit
was that, quite apart from his ability as a staff officer, he
really made his officers think for themselves. T. E. Lawrence
wrote in one of his published letters, 'What staggers me is the
incuriosity of most officers.' 'Monty', by analysing each
exercise in the presence of all his officers and making outspoken comments on senior officers, riveted their attention

on the lessons to be learned and ensured that on the next
exercise everyone would constantly ask himself, 'What will
"Monty" say we should be doing now?' There is no doubt
that 'Monty' himself learned a great deal from the short
campaign in France and Belgium—mainly from his opponents, then at the peak of their form.

'Monty' had not yet developed the characteristic which
has subsequently got him into trouble, namely, a love of
publicity. A certain senior general once said to me of Leslie
Hore-Belisha, 'He is a good War Secretary but the greatest
crime in his eyes is for anyone to get between him and a
press photographer.' I am convinced that 'Monty' always
knew what he was doing with the Press and that he used
them as a deliberate act of policy. When later in the war I
was sent from the War Office to Liverpool to report on the
comments made by returning Eighth Army veterans of the
50th and other divisions, I found that their main complaint
had nothing to do with pay or food or beer or any of the
expected subjects. What they wanted to know was why the
7th Armoured Division and the 51st Highland Division got
all the publicity. None of these men objected to the publicity
given to the Eighth Army Commander. On the contrary,
most of them realised that he was probably seeking publicity
for himself in the interests of his men.

Long afterwards he made a speech in which he deplored
the lack of leadership in the national life. It was featured
prominently in the Sunday newspapers. I accordingly put a
question on the order paper to the Prime Minister on the
subject—my point being that it was wrong for the Chief of
the Imperial General Staff to make public utterances which
could be so obviously interpreted in a political sense. 'Monty'
expressed his regrets to the Prime Minister for the purposes
of the reply which the Prime Minister gave to my question.
When I walked out of the Chamber, I was stopped by
A. V. Alexander, then Minister of Defence, who was chatting
with the Prime Minister. 'Ah', he said, 'I have an invitation
from the Field-Marshal for you. When we talked to him
about this he said, "Blackburn was one of my officers. Tell
him to come and have lunch with me." ' Attlee said, 'You

know the Field-Marshal had not the slightest idea that his speech would attract such publicity.' I was too satisfied with the result of my question to inform Attlee and 'Albert Victorious', as Alexander was sometimes called, that by then the Field-Marshal knew ten times as much about publicity as both of them put together. It must, however, be almost unique for a man to have such personality that after indirectly attacking the Prime Minister in a manner which he could not defend, he should in effect turn that Prime Minister's Minister of Defence into a messenger with an invitation to lunch to a young M.P. Evidently both Attlee and Alexander accepted 'Monty' at his own valuation, than which one could hardly go higher. The one man he really respected in the Labour Government was the man who matched his own egotism, Ernest Bevin.

During the 1940-1941 winter 'Monty' certainly trained us hard. On one bitterly cold day he made most of the 3rd Division march across Salisbury Plain. One battalion marched sixty-seven miles in thirty hours; all of them marched well over fifty miles. That he made senior officers do six-mile runs and when warned that they might die said, 'Let them die', is not an apocryphal story. He had an essential quality of genius—absolute ruthlessness in the attainment of the object.

As I was the only solicitor in the Brigade there was great demand for my services as defending officer. A number of the men I defended were acquitted. One day the Colonel of another battalion asked me to dinner in his mess, and afterwards said, 'Blackburn, I have a really first-class Company Quarter-Master Sergeant, whom I cannot afford to lose. But the silly ass was caught by the Military Police at Waterloo Station the other day going on leave with seven pounds of butter and three pounds of tea in his kit-bag. I have had to remand him for court-martial, but please get him off if you can.' He had made a statement to the Military Police containing some absurdities, but I was able to get this excluded on technical grounds at the trial (over which a friend of mine presided). I did not call the C.Q.M.S. as a witness but relied on the submission that the evidence was inconclusive. He

BX

was acquitted. A fortnight later, to my surprise, I received a
present of a box of cigars. By then I had become Brigade
Intelligence Officer. One evening during an exercise I
handed the box round the mess. The Brigadier left the table
to talk to General Montgomery, who had arrived to find out
how 'the battle' was progressing. When he came back there
was a twinkle in his eye. 'Blackburn, the General has given
me an order that on account of your high quality as a staff
officer you cannot be spared in future to act as defending
officer in any case.' 'Then, sir', I replied, 'I regret that there
will be no more boxes of cigars to hand round the mess.'
It was a rather naughty joke as the Brigadier would not have
accepted a cigar if he had known that the C.Q.M.S. had
given them to me. 'One day', he replied, 'that tongue of
yours is going to get you into a lot of trouble.' He was right.

During 1940 I came into constant touch with the Local
Defence Volunteers—the forerunners of the Home Guard.
They must have been one of the finest forces of men ever
assembled. Former brigadier-generals and colonels served
cheerfully in the ranks. A former army commander was
happy to be in command of a company. I was once deputed
to give a lesson in tactics to a platoon, some of whom had
been in action fifteen years before I was born. Fortunately,
as a result of being the constant companion of Colonel
Given, I did know the answer to some military problems.
But no young subaltern could have had a more understanding and friendly audience. If the Germans had been able
to invade, they would never have been safe at any time of
the day or night from attacks of one kind or another from
these men, so many of whom had spent their lives soldiering.
It is fashionable to deride Colonel Blimps, but I have generally found that men with the King's and the Queen's medal
ribbons on their tunics are a great deal more agile in mind
than their children and grandchildren. When I went to
Greece at the height of the so-called civil war in early 1948,
it seemed to me that the worst advisers of the Greek army
were those who still thought in terms of the last war, when
they should have been thinking in terms of the last war but
two. The Boer War veteran, Sir Charles Wickham, whom

Bevin had sent out to re-organise the Greek police, had sounder ideas than our military missions.

More nonsense has probably been talked about the Battle of Britain than about any other battle in history. It has been suggested and widely believed that in 1940 Britain was utterly defenceless and that Churchill bluffed the Germans into refraining from attacking us. It has even been generally assumed that the loss of the battle in the air would have entailed the likelihood of a successful invasion. The German military and naval experts knew better. I have heard Churchill indignantly deny more than once that he was indispensable during this period. My own Division, the 3rd Division, was completely re-equipped by June 16th, more than three months before the Germans could have mounted their attack for which the earliest date was September 22nd. If they had suffered no loss from the Navy and the Air Force—an inconceivable assumption—the attack would have landed forces amounting to a third of nine divisions. Even if Folkestone and Dover had been captured immediately—a most unlikely event—the ports would not have been able to supply half the needs of the assault force. In fact, of course, the Navy would have intercepted the supplies. We have only to consider the immense difficulties the British-American forces met in 1944, when we had absolute naval and air superiority and superb equipment for our invasion forces, to realise that a hastily planned and equipped German invasion in late September or early October 1940, with the British Navy still in command of the sea round our coasts, could have had only one possible result—utter failure within a week—by which time the supplies of such forces as had managed to penetrate our powerful beach defences would have run out. All this in no way detracts from Churchill's superb leadership and immortal eloquence (particularly in the speech he delivered with his execrable but endearing French accent to the French people).

CHAPTER IV

Politics in Wartime

I DO not think that there was anything in my life which I wanted more than a decoration for gallantry in the war. After the campaign in 1940, I was bitterly disappointed not to receive one. The fact that I never again had the chance to distinguish myself in action was partly due to drink, although I would never have admitted it at the time. In 1941 I was the adjutant of a unit of my Regiment which had been converted into Light Anti-Aircraft. One day in 1942, after I had had a few drinks, I returned for lunch to our headquarters to find that a mobilisation order had been issued for our Division. My delight at this event added to the exhilaration produced by the drink was my downfall. I jumped on a motor-bike and hurried off to Brigade Headquarters, only to meet with an accident which sent me to hospital for several months and kept me out of the war for much longer. The wound in my leg did not heal for over a year. Although no blame was ever attached to me or even remotely suggested as attributable to me, I knew in my heart that if I had been completely sober I would not have come to grief.

This accident changed the whole course of my life, for in the enforced idleness caused by my convalescence, my thoughts turned more and more to politics in which I had always been interested. In 1943 I fought a bye-election and from that time onwards it was inevitable that politics would play a great part in my life. By then I had gone far to the left. To explain how this change had taken place in me, as in so many other young men like myself, would have been easier at that time than now when so much has changed in the world.

I had been brought up as a Tory. The political and economic doctrines of the Conservative Party were dinned into my ears from the time when I was a young boy. My father was President of the local Conservative Club and a man of considerable influence in local politics. He even managed to get me a seat at the age of fourteen for the meeting of the Conservative Grand Council at which Stanley Baldwin propounded the unsuccessful election slogan, 'Safety First'. Baldwin's photograph held an honoured place in our home and my mother never forgot to send him a telegram on his birthday. Although Churchill was greatly admired, Baldwin and later Chamberlain were revered as the high priests of Conservatism. In 1938 I had become an occasional visitor to the Speakers' Class at the Conservatives' Head Office.

Foreign affairs interested me most. My ignorance of European affairs was so abysmal that I believed that the Munich settlement would be the end of Hitler's territorial ambitions in Europe. Certainly there were few people inside or outside Parliament who opposed Munich at the time. If Chamberlain had requested the King to dissolve Parliament and asked for an election mandate for his policy of appeasement he would have been returned to power with an immense majority. March 1939 brought a complete change. Chamberlain had agreed to guarantee the frontiers of the reconstituted Czechoslovakia, but when Hitler marched into Prague, his immediate reaction was feeble if not actually dishonest. At the Speakers' Class that night I denounced it as such and was surprised to find about half those present in agreement with me. Chamberlain spoke strongly a day or two later and even referred to 'the sickening technique' of the secret police and the concentration camp, but he gave the impression that he was following and not leading public opinion. In common with a large number of other people I left the Conservative Party and went to Transport House. 'Dick' Windle, the Assistant National Agent, told me that many young men like myself were joining the Labour Party on account of disillusionment with Tory foreign policy, but he clearly had his doubts whether we were likely to remain long in it, unless we also accepted its domestic policy.

It was the war which was responsible for the great shift

leftwards in the opinions of so many people of whom I was one. It is probably a mistake to suppose that the main reason was the failure of the appeasement policy. The record of the Labour Party on this issue was far too dubious to justify the assertion that 'the left had been right'. Their failure to support conscription three months before the outbreak of war contrasts strangely with their subsequent record of continuing it indefinitely in peace time. Undoubt-edly Churchill was the one man who had proved consistently right over both the threat of Nazism and the need for rearmament—and he appeared to be on the right wing of the Conservative Party.

The two main factors which influenced me—and I believe many others—were the disgracefully low pay and allowances in the armed forces and the apparent exposure of the falsity of Conservative beliefs about the Soviet Union. About the latter we were to some extent wrong, although most Tories had made themselves ridiculous by their gross under-estimates of the strength of the Soviet Union. But there was no excuse whatever for the Conservative Government's apparent unconcern for the welfare of servicemen and their families. It made many people like myself feel that their toleration of mass unemployment had been due to similar heartlessness. Later, pay and allowances improved, but when they did so it appeared to be under pressure from the left.

I was approached in 1940 by the Haldane Society, a Society of Socialist Lawyers, to write a small book to be called *The Soldier's Guide*. I did so, using my own name but omitting any reference to my military status. I knew that if I asked the Army Council for permission to publish, I would either be refused it or made to wait for so long that the project would fall through. The first edition of ten thousand copies sold out quickly, and it finally went into four editions. Here again I was impressed by the fact that it was the left in politics which appeared most anxious to help servicemen to protect themselves. An attitude common among some Conservatives was that the less the soldier knew about his rights the better. No doubt the barrack-room lawyer is a nuisance and his own worst enemy, but to keep soldiers ignorant of their rights is very wrong, particularly in view of the fact that a proportion of officers allow their authority to go to their heads. 'The supreme proof of virtue is to possess boundless power without abusing it.' Very few people can withstand so exacting a test.

Before the Germans invaded the Soviet Union I had become convinced that our military experts greatly under-estimated its strength and I said so openly on many occasions. In fairness I must admit that my views were treated with good-humoured tolerance, and that I was allowed to be 'Bolshie' without suffering any disadvantages therefrom. The Germans in fact gained great victories in 1941, but far greater victories had been confidently predicted for them by officers who should have known better—including 'Monty'. Feelings of gratitude to the Russian people for their heroic resistance were widespread. There was also the awkward fact that the Government had cold-shouldered the Soviet Union at the time of Munich and that it might well have appeared to Stalin that our design was to give Hitler a free hand for his projected drive into the Ukraine. Probably few people really attributed such Machiavellian motives to Chamberlain, but his manifest ignorance of foreign affairs reflected discredit on his docile supporters. It is an unpleasant thought that a great many votes may have swung to Labour in 1945 because of the triumph of Soviet arms and the belief that it proved the efficacy of a planned economy. Churchill himself contributed to spreading pro-Soviet sympathy. He even warned Vernon Bartlett not to write in time of war about the more sombre side of the Soviet picture. Pro-Soviet books such as those of the Dean of Canterbury, D. N. Pritt and Sir Richard Acland had huge sales and for the more critical reader there was the vast erudition of Sidney and Beatrice Webb's two volumes full of similar enthusiasm. If indeed the Soviet Union had genuinely tried to co-operate with the West, it would have had great support among the masses after the war and could have thereby directly influenced British policy.

If it had not been for the accident which sent me to

hospital in 1942 and kept me out of the army for a year, I should never have been able to take any part in war-time politics and I should never have become a Member of Parliament. While convalescing near Ashford in Kent, I went to a public meeting held by Sir Richard Acland, leader of Commonwealth. Rather rudely, I asked him whether he had read H. G. Wells' characteristically caustic comment: 'Sir Richard Acland preaches a kind of Christian Communism, but I notice that in the meantime he retains his title, his investments and his clothes.' As a result of a discussion which followed this question we struck up an immediate friendship. He made me a candidate at a bye-election at Watford. The announcement of the former was deliberately postponed until the result of the bye-election had been declared. Although ineffective in the House of Commons, and somewhat erratic in his opinions, Acland has played a valuable part in public life because of his courage and sincerity. The series of bye-elections which he fought should have warned the Government that it was getting out of touch with the electorate. It must have had some effect in modifying the attitude of the Government to subjects such as service pay and allowances.

To fight a bye-election in time of war was a fascinating experience. One or two bye-elections were won by independent candidates immediately following defeats in the field. The Watford bye-election was at a time when the North African campaign was being successfully brought to a conclusion. The Government had satisfactory achievements to their credit in the military and diplomatic field. Churchill sent a telegram to my opponent hoping that he might be spared the distraction of a 'futile contest'. In such circumstances it says a great deal for the independence of mind of the British public and for their sense of fairness that throughout this campaign, although I was fighting Group-Captain Helmore, a famous broadcaster supported by the three main political parties, my meetings were well attended and my incessant talks on the loud-speaker almost always received courteously and without interference. The meetings were often enthusiastic. I was somewhat alarmed by the applause which greeted questions like the following: 'Will the candidate if returned seek to have Stanley Baldwin and the other guilty men impeached and hanged?'

The result of the bye-election was the return of Group-Captain Helmore by the unexpectedly small majority of 2,000. It was a moral defeat for the Conservatives, who would have lost if there had been a new register and the outlying dormitory areas like Rickmansworth had not still been included in the constituency. Moreover, after I had stressed for some time as the first plank in my platform 'The Beveridge Report to be implemented now', my opponent yielded to this initiative and announced that he was unequivocally in favour of the Beveridge Report and wished a start to be made immediately on implementing it. Government policy at the time was to refer it for further consideration to official committees of various kinds. The House of Commons did not suit my gallant opponent, who distinguished himself on D-Day by broadcasting from a bomber over Caen. It is a pity that men of his calibre do not show in the political field the courage and skill which they possess. Churchill was his hero and he was no Tory at heart. He would have made an excellent progressive Member of Parliament, particularly as he was an inventor. But the game of Party politics did not appeal to him.

One point in Acland's speeches which greatly appealed to the independent voter was his statement that no candidate sponsored by Commonwealth would ever be required or expected to vote otherwise than in accordance with his conscience. No doubt such specific latitude could not be granted by the main political parties, but they could much more frequently leave issues to a free vote of the House of Commons. This would raise the prestige of Parliament without undermining the authority of the Government. Certainly when a free vote is allowed in the House of Commons, the members afterwards claim that an unusually good debate occurs. There is something very sad about the thought that all the speeches delivered in the House of Commons on issues of major policy are beating the air. They cannot hope to change the actual decision by vote. They

may have influence and effect but it is a foregone conclusion
that the Government will win the day.

When the Watford bye-election was over I advised my
supporters, with Acland's consent, to prepare for the General
Election by joining the Labour Party. (A few of them were,
of course, members already.) I saw 'Dick' Windle again and
became friendly with him and with other members of the
staff at Transport House. Before long I was accepted on the
panel of Labour candidates. While I was at the War Office
and the Staff College I was able to keep in touch with a
number of people who were in positions of some influence in
the Labour Party, and to learn something about the Labour
movement and its background. Windle and Shepherd, the
National Agent, were anxious to recruit servicemen in the
Labour Party, being well aware that the only Labour M.P.
who saw active service in the Second World War was my
friend F. J. Bellenger, with whom I wrote a booklet on
exservicemen's problems. Shepherd, when informing me of
his acceptance of my request to be a candidate, said, 'You
will learn that the Labour Party is conservative with a small
"c". We must remember that before long we shall be the
Government of the country.' These two men played an
immense part in ensuring that the 1945 Parliament was far
more nearly a representative cross-section of the electorate
than any previous Parliament. It was a great pity that many
young men who would have been excellent Members of
Parliament never had the chance to be considered as candidates because they were serving abroad. In general, the most
adventurous and patriotic young men of this period who
did not belong to ancient political families, excluded themselves from the post-war Parliament by their concentration
on the war. It is to their credit that they did so, but the
country may well prove to have been the loser in the end.
Most of the present Labour hierarchy accepted the view
that their services in non-combatant positions were too
valuable to justify their volunteering for action. They were
probably right, but as a result they missed experiences
which might have opened their eyes to aspects of life which
are a closed book to them and which might have predisposed

their minds against excessive respect for official files. Conservatives are conformists by political faith. Unfortunately, most leading Socialist M.P.s are conformists by experience, having graduated through the trade unions or the co-operative movement or the Civil Service. Never has it been more important to have men of independent and adventurous mind in positions of political leadership, and never have such men been so unlikely to engage in politics or, if they did so, to attain those positions.

I had some idea even during the war that this was so. There were two men whom I met in the Services and introduced to Bellenger who proposed them with me as candidates. Moreover, in both cases I introduced them to their constituencies. Their names were John Freeman and Woodrow Wyatt and they were both staff officers.

I met John Freeman while I was at the Staff College. He became eventually the junior Minister who resigned with Aneuran Bevan and Harold Wilson over the issues of the scale of rearmament in 1951—and he was right over the issue itself. When I met him he was the most characteristic staff officer one could hope to meet—with perfect manners, a smart and handsome appearance, a command of army clichés and a considerable experience as Deputy Assistant Quarter-Master General in the 7th Armoured Division in North Africa. I was amazed to hear him say to me one night in the mess at the Staff College—where my left-wing views were well known—'I have been a Socialist ever since I was at Oxford and I am a more convinced Socialist today than ever. I hardly expect you to believe me in view of my behaviour here.' Of course, the word 'Socialist' can mean anything or nothing. Stalin and Hitler, Bevin and Cripps, claimed to be Socialists at the same time as they attacked one another. Even so, I knew what he meant and the record shows that he was telling the truth. He was in Germany when his wife and I appeared on his behalf before the Watford Labour Party and secured the nomination.

Woodrow Wyatt was an entirely different character. I met him just before D-Day because I had to defend an officer of my old Division on a most unusual charge. This officer had suddenly decided that it was contrary to the word of God for him to take any part in war. He had had an undoubtedly genuine religious conversion, made all the more intense by his love for a simple and beautiful young girl who shared his beliefs. The whole affair was the more extraordinary because he was the only intellectual whom I had previously met in the Army, and one does not associate such sudden emotional changes with men of his type. The Judge Advocate General, a Lieutenant-Colonel, who prosecuted, informed me that the young officer would get at least twelve months and even made public insinuations against his personal courage—although he clearly had no intention of ever demonstrating his own. To their credit the Court decided that he should be dismissed the Service— which was the sentence for which I asked. All the members of the Court knew that they would be on the invasion beach on D-Day and the President was killed. Lack of generosity towards genuine conscientious objectors, as towards the captured enemy, is the hallmark of those who are willing to leave the actual fighting to others.

Woodrow Wyatt, a young dark man in spectacles, was obviously inquisitive and intelligent. At the time he was a Liberal but was perfectly prepared to join the Labour Party if he would thereby gain the chance of getting into Parliament. I introduced him to Bellenger and we both proposed him for the panel of Parliamentary candidates. My Birmingham agent and I then introduced him to the Aston Labour Party, which duly adopted him. When he got into Parliament he helped make a name for himself by constant attacks on his former sponsor, Bellenger, then Secretary of State for War. Bellenger was hurt but had too much dignity to strike back. Wyatt joined the 'Keep Left Group', but in 1951 when Bevan, Wilson and Freeman left the Labour Government he attacked them with contempt as well as bitterness, saying that they had not the slightest idea why they were leaving the Government. In fact, of course, as Churchill later admitted, Bevan's statement that the £4,700,000 defence programme was not only grossly extravagant but actually beyond the capacity of industry to

implement, was perfectly correct. Attlee rewarded Wyatt for
attacking Bevan by giving him a post as Under-Secretary for
War. Such are the rewards for those who place Party before
personal loyalties.

The constituency in which I was adopted as candidate was
the Kings Norton Division, comprising a good deal of
industry to the south of Birmingham, including the Austin
works and Cadbury's. I was recommended to it by Harold
Laski, who enjoyed a reputation among constituency parties
which matched his international reputation. Long after I
had reached a political position—particularly in relation to
Communism—far removed from him, he continued to pay a
substantial annual sum anonymously to my constituency
party. Although he loved to talk about revolution, he was a
most kindly and generous man. He was always willing to
produce references and literature which told in favour of the
case made out by his opponents. For instance, he had
acquired and lent me the verbatim account of the famous
Moscow state trials in which Vishinsky and the Soviet leaders
reached inconceivable depths of degradation. This was not
only horrifying but fascinating, as it contained passages
such as that where Vishinsky, made to appear a novice by
Bukharin's references to political philosophy, rebuked him
with the words:

VISHINSKY: You are on trial as a criminal, not as a
philosopher.

BUKHARIN: But a criminal may also be a philosopher.
Yagoda, former chief of the O.G.P.U., after confessing to
helping to poison Maxim Gorki, Stalin's closest friend,
boggled at two confessions even more absurd than the usual
confessions being extorted from the wretched prisoners, and
won his way despite an adjournment, clearly because he had
threatened to expose the methods by which such confessions
had been obtained. No one knew better than he.

Laski, regarded as an extreme Socialist, had even written
a book on *Liberty in the Modern State*. I lent the state trials
account to Churchill (who returned it to Laski), secretly
hoping to be present at an encounter between them, as Laski
was really a great admirer of Churchill, but it was not to be.

Laski, apart from his fine human qualities, remains an
enigma. He knew all about the horrors of Soviet Communism;
he understood the enormous power of the bureaucracy in
the modern state; he saw that the freedom in which liberals
believed was being destroyed all over the world; yet he
regarded it almost as his mission to persuade those who felt
like him, that all these things must be endured for the general
advance of humanity. I very rapidly came to believe the
exact opposite, yet my political sponsor in Kings Norton
continued to support me as a person.

It was quite plain even in 1944 that there was mounting
enthusiasm on the left. Yet of all the Labour leaders that I
met in Transport House, in Parliament, and at Labour
conferences, none but Aneurin Bevan regarded it as remotely
possible that Labour could attain a sweeping victory at the
polls so long as Churchill fulfilled expectations and led the
Conservatives at the General Election. Even Ernest Bevin
implicitly indicated his own forecast of the future by saying
that he was considering whether after the war he should
enter the lists of those who control newspapers. As is well
known, the *Daily Mirror* and *Sunday Pictorial* group had no
controlling shareholder. Indeed, Sir John Ellerman, whose
main public interest is in the People's Dispensary for Sick
Animals, is the largest shareholder. Cecil King, then Deputy
Chairman and now Chairman of the group, a nephew of
Lord Northcliffe, told me that he would be glad to know
whether Bevin would take an interest in the group by buying
up shares on terms to be agreed. I saw Bevin at Transport
House and discussed the matter with him at some length.
He agreed that it was well worthy of consideration, although
he despised the *Daily Mirror* and had been the Minister
mainly responsible for its being warned during the war.
He well knew that if handled in a statesmanlike way, it
could have great influence. However, he sent me a message
a few days later that 'his friends' were not interested in
financing such a proposition. The strange fact is that 'his
friends' were very wealthy Jews—and Bevin was always
alleged to be anti-Semitic.

At the Blackpool Conference of the Labour Party which

became the pre-election Conference, Churchill offered to continue the coalition after the war. He had first made this offer verbally to Attlee and had received the impression that it might well be acceptable. Attlee in turn submitted it to the National Executive of the Labour Party where it was supported by Bevin and three others. Characteristically Attlee himself kept silent at the Executive meeting. It was already obvious that if the Conservatives suffered from having too dominant a leader, the Labour Party suffered from the very opposite defect. Later, through having the authority of the office of Prime Minister for so long, Attlee acquired the reputation of having some personality. But on this first occasion when I met him and often afterwards, I felt astonished that such a man should be the leader of a Party containing men of such outstanding ability as Bevin, Cripps, Bevan and Morrison. The fact that he was the leader was a pointer to the future. Moreover, for a time at least he suited the mood of the public which, after five years of the leadership of a man of overpowering personality and vivid imagination, liked to revert to the Baldwin-Chamberlain type of unpretentious Prime Ministers with reputations for soundness and Party loyalty.

At the 1945 Election it was soon apparent that the revulsion of feeling against the Tories was at its height. But more serious for their electoral chances was the widespread understanding of the point that it was very unfair that the Tories should pin their hopes on Churchill, when Churchill had been their bugbear immediately before the war, and when the majority of Tories had voted in May 1940 to keep Chamberlain in power. The main credit for the fact that Churchill became Prime Minister was due to the Labour and Liberal Parties, and his own conduct in attacking them, particularly in the 'Gestapo' speech, seemed churlish, ungenerous and out of character. 'Now he really is the prisoner of the Tories', some said; others, 'Now he has come out in his true colours.' The name of Winston Churchill lost its magic in a few weeks—inside this country but not abroad. Having got to know him so well later, I came to understand that the 'Gestapo' speech was very much his own and represented his

profound conviction that real Socialism means ownership
by the State of the means of production, distribution and
exchange, and that the appalling inefficiencies which would
result would create conditions in which a secret police would
be needed. It is certainly true that totalitarian governments faced with internal or external disaster invariably
allege widespread treason and sabotage and find it necessary to manufacture scapegoats. The tendency was seen in a
mild fashion in 1947 when so many Socialists sought to put
the blame for the financial crisis on 'Tory sabotage' and on
'the spivs'. Many of the rank and file really believed this and
could see nothing incongruous in the idea that Birmingham
industrialists would deliberately lose export markets and
frustrate production in order to discredit the Socialist
Government. All this cannot, however, excuse Churchill's
major political blunders in the 1945 Election or acquit him
of the charge that he treated his loyal colleagues of the
wartime administration, the very men who had really put
him into 10 Downing Street, with scant consideration.

Although at the previous election there had been a
Conservative majority of 5,800, I was absolutely confident
of victory. The Kings Norton Divisional Labour Party was a
very live Party and was soon to have in its largest ward,
Northfield, a record membership for the Midlands—one
voter in every nine a paying member. In this and the subsequent General Election we actually made a profit, paying all
the election expenses out of contributions made and having
two or three hundred pounds to spare for the forthcoming
municipal elections. There were row on row of houses in
some areas on the front windows of every one of which my
photograph appeared. My majority was 12,800—a turnover
of more than 18,000 votes. The enthusiasm at the victory
meeting was intense. The hall seemed to be full of shining eyes
aglow with the sight of the promised land. My knowledge
of the Labour leaders and particularly my brief acquain-
tanceship with the leader of the Party made me feel
sure that a rude awakening was coming before long. They had
put their trust in an organisation. To place one's trust in
any man is dangerous enough, but to have blind faith in an

organisation is the surest road to trouble. Collective man has less conscience than the individuals that compose him. The victory, as Aneurin Bevan had prophesied, was a victory over the Tories, a repudiation of the record of the Conservative Party. Although the Labour Party had fought on a precise programme drafted by Herbert Morrison, it was not this programme which won the election. It was the memories of mass unemployment, of Britain's desperate plight in 1940 and of the Conservative Party's apparent reluctance to implement the Beveridge Report, combined with the feeling that after fourteen years of Conservative domination of the House of Commons, a change was long overdue, that swept the Labour Party into its triumph. We paid tribute to the pioneers, the men who had preached Socialism when their reward was insults even from their fellow working-men. But they were dead long ago and they would have had little in common with the Whitehall planners who now saw the lights go green.

CHAPTER V

The Honeymoon Year

THE overwhelming Labour victory of 1945 could have been an event of immense significance for the world as well as for Britain. Labour propagandists had promised a peaceful resolution in the event of victory. The fact that the overwhelming majority of the votes of the men who had done the fighting went to Labour immensely strengthened its moral position and enhanced its prestige. There can be little doubt that if Attlee and his colleagues had been genuine revolutionaries determined to transfer power from those who wielded it, they could have succeeded. For some time after the 1945 victory even the Tory press produced only muffled criticism of the Government. The House of Lords would never have risked suicide by exercising its right to veto legislation. It did not even do so in 1947, when the Labour Government at the nadir of its fortunes produced an Act of Parliament which gave it unlimited powers to direct labour and requisition property. It certainly would not have opposed any measures introduced in 1945 or 1946 which could by any stretch of the imagination have been interpreted as necessary to show whether Socialism could really work.

Labour, in short, had the opportunity to do what it liked and to show what it meant by Socialism. *What in fact happened was that it increased the wealth of the wealthy and put even more power into the hands of those who already possessed it—the big industrialists, the civil servants, and the huge established trade unions.* The discerning observer has seen this process continued by the Conservatives. That does not excuse Labour, as they represented themselves to be the advocates of change, whereas the Conservatives are by their very title opponents

of change. In claiming to have effected a revolution, one
considers whom the Labour leaders and their followers—
including myself—thought they could convince, apart from
themselves. It is easy to persuade oneself of the truth of what
one really wants to say. In Parliament where Party feelings
and loyalties run strong and the lobbies are full of constituents who are anxious to be as friendly as possible to their
member, it is difficult for him to judge (even if he be the
rare member trying to judge) the reactions of the fair-
minded man or woman who puts the interests of his country
and his neighbours before the attractions of a political faith
or Party loyalty. These people rarely write to their M.P.
or attend his meetings. Sometimes, I suspect, they are so
disgusted that they do not vote at all—and are denounced
by Party hacks whose docility is a disgrace to the democracy
about which they perorate.

During the whole of the first year after the election
victory, the popularity of Labour remained near its peak.
The immediate raising of the old age pension from 10s. to
26s., accompanied by the National Insurance Bill promising
'security from the cradle to the grave', persuaded those who
had voted Labour that their representatives were keeping
faith with them. When Hugh Dalton assured a delighted
Labour Conference that he would find the money for such
purposes with a song in his heart, he struck the right note.
Afterwards he was subjected to cruel criticism on account of
this remark, but at the time it commanded the support of
most decent people in the country. They felt that it was high
time that we had a Chancellor of the Exchequer who was a
human being rather than what Aneurin Bevan called a
'desiccated calculating machine'. Moreover Dalton had had
great immediate success with his cheap money policy,
borrowing hundreds of millions of pounds from the City at
the rate of $2\frac{1}{2}$ per cent. Again, it has since been suggested
that this was dishonest. Every change in the bank rate puts
money into the pockets of some people and takes it away
from others. A dear money policy such as that adopted later
is for obvious reasons congenial to wealthy people and
uncongenial to the 'little man'. It seems self-evident that if

it is possible to maintain a cheap money policy, it benefits the country which has to pay less for the money it borrows, and small businessmen generally who can borrow money at a cheaper rate. Its main disadvantage is that it is inflationary in effect. It was for that reason that Labour later raised the bank rate. But it seems utterly unfair to suggest that one political Party can put the bank rate up honestly and that it is dishonest for another political Party to put it down. Indeed, ideally a cheap money policy is best.

Of course, Dalton and his future were the key to the whole situation. The fears that the Labour Government would not enjoy the confidence of the City and would in some mysterious way be brought down by evil men in toppers and morning suits had vanished. The real trouble was to come from our balance-of-payments problem and from the inadequacy and harsh terms of the American loan. But during the honeymoon year this was not apparent. It is therefore interesting to analyse the behaviour of the Labour Government during this period when they really could have been revolutionary.

Two or three days after the Labour victory, Dalton held a dinner for twelve young men (including John Wilmot) who were friends of his and supposed to be the new hopes of the Party. They included Gaitskell, Wilson, Callaghan, Crossman, Evan Durbin, and others including myself. Few Ministerial appointments had been made: Wilmot had not yet been made Minister of Supply. Dalton asked us for suggestions as to the course of action which should be taken by the Government in order to maintain the impetus of the election victory. The fact that we were to proceed immediately with the nationalisation of coal and then the railways was a foregone conclusion. But these measures, while greatly affecting a few constituencies, left most constituencies more or less untouched. The full implementation of our social security proposals and the introduction of the Health Service were popular measures with a wide effect, but they could not fairly be classed as distinctively Labour policies. Indeed, the foundations for them were laid by Liberal Governments, and the Conservative members of the National Government of 1940-1945 under Churchill had committed themselves in principle to acceptance of such policies. It might pertinently be asked what distinctively Labour policies there were affecting industry as a whole. That we might retain controls longer than the Conservatives would, appeared inherent in the political outlook of Labour. But this represented no more than a slight change of emphasis, a difference in degree but certainly not in kind between Labour and Conservative policies.

I suggested that the Government should take practical steps designed to associate the workers and their representatives with production and with the responsibilities of management. In particular I advocated that industry generally should be approached to agree that on the boards of companies employing large numbers of men, two men should be appointed from the workers themselves or their trade union representatives. This proposal was received in sceptical silence. Yet something similar has been done in Germany since the war—and the record of German industry is well-known. Moreover, even in Britain there had been joint production committees in many factories for the purpose of increasing the war effort. When later I took the adjournment of the House of Commons on the subject of joint production machinery, I received an answer from the Government which paid lip-service to the principle in question, but showed that little or nothing was being done to put it into effect. I found just as much interest among Conservatives as among Socialists—with the sole exception of the Post Office Workers Union. In fact, the shop steward movement itself, from which joint production machinery largely originated, was regarded with suspicion by many trade unionists, because there were so many Communist or near-Communist shop stewards during the war. This attitude of suspicion and even hostility towards what should have been the most practical and progressive element in the Labour ranks was the cause of endless trouble. The rigid, bureaucratic outlook of many trade unionists, themselves men of principle and goodwill, drove many men who should have been their allies into the arms of the friends of the Communists. The Transport and General Workers

Union had a habit of addressing letters to its members
signed (literally) with a rubber stamp—even on matters of
great personal importance to them, such as claims for work-
men's compensation. Trade union representatives constantly use the word 'instruct' in relation to their men who
really should be regarded as their employers. The fact that
they are for the most part grossly underpaid and frequently
earn less money than most of the men on whose behalf they
are negotiating, is not widely known. It is inevitable that
they get more and more out of touch with their workers.
The trade unionists of this country are outstandingly honest
and incorruptible, but they badly need an injection of vigour
and imagination to save them from appearing to the rank
and file of the workers as paid hacks with a conservative
attitude to the problems of today and tomorrow.

The hostility latent in Government circles to the shop
steward movement and the subjection of first-class Ministers
to their senior civil servants was soon made plain to me.
Austins built a shadow factory during the war for the production of bomber aircraft. It was known as Austin Aero and
had a production-line a quarter of a mile long. It was
admittedly one of the very finest factories in the country, but
its shop stewards had made themselves unpopular in many
quarters because of the strength of their left-wing tendencies.
When the end of the war came, negotiations proceeded
between the Government and the management of Austins
as to the future use of the factory. Mr Leonard Lord (as he
then was) sought to obtain certain concessions which were
not granted him. The Government then decided to requisition Austin Aero for the storage of naval guns. When I first
heard about it from the shop stewards, I could not believe
that anything so absurd could be proposed even by the
gentlemen of Whitehall. However, it was confirmed to me
by Mr Lord both that the Government were requisitioning
Austin Aero for the storage of naval guns, and that if they
would abandon their plans, he would use the factory for
motor-car production. Privately he informed me of plans
to manufacture a new Austin Seven.

With the support of the shop stewards I obtained an

official interview with Sir Stafford Cripps, President of the Board of Trade, and Sir Philip Warter, then one of his chief civil servants but now Chairman of Associated British Picture Corporation, Ltd, the Anglo-American company controlling the A.B.C. circuit and Pathé. Cripps was most courteous and patient, as usual. His manners were those of a somewhat frigid aristocrat with a gleam of missionary zeal in his eyes. Reflecting on his pre-war activities as sponsor of the Socialist League and advocate of a Popular Front, I anticipated no difficulty in persuading him to reverse a decision the sole justification for which could be the political motive of destroying the Communist cells in the factory. That one of the best factories in Britain should be used to store naval guns, many of which were obsolete, seemed incredible. Mr Lord had suggested that it would be better to consign the guns to the custody of Neptune rather than that they should impede Britain's industrial recovery. Another naval war seemed a remote possibility. Moreover, some method could surely be found to store guns without taking up such valuable space.

Cripps listened quietly and appreciatively and turned almost appealingly to Sir Philip Warter. 'Could we not change our plans, if Lord is willing to use the factory for the production of cars?' Sir Philip Warter turned down the suggestion flat. He said that to change plans would cause administrative chaos. The guns were in a number of small factories which would be freed for industry by the transfer to Austin Aero. Cripps turned to me and said, 'I would like to have helped you but I must accept the advice of Sir Philip Warter.' Some years after, I met Sir Philip Warter when he had returned to the business world and I reminded him of this interview. Having long left Whitehall he no longer sought to defend the decision then made. No doubt it was more convenient for the civil servants at Whitehall that no last-minute change should be made in their plans. But the attitude of Cripps as Minister was utterly indefensible. He could see that I could hardly believe my ears and said a trifle coldly, 'Of course you can take the adjournment of the House on the subject, but it will not change my position.'

I fully intended to do so, but Mr Lord was so exasperated by the whole business that he said it was best to forget about it. If we had so incompetent a Government he did not wish to be the first to expose its deficiencies, which would be seen soon enough by everybody. Labour was then at the height of its popularity and my own supporters did not wish me to make an exposure of the weakness of a leading Labour Minister at such a time. I have always regretted that I accepted their advice.

Another illustration of the myopia of even the most distinguished civil servants arose in connection with greyhound-racing. I was on the Committee of the Borrowing Control and Guarantees Bill which when enacted required Treasury consent for certain types of borrowing and investment, particularly public issues. I noticed that there were two offers for sale of shares in greyhound-racing concerns. It seemed extraordinary that the Treasury should have given its consent to these, and on enquiry I found that the Treasury regarded offers for sale as being outside the ambit of the Act on the academic ground that they did not create 'new money' in the technical sense of the term. I had many arguments with Evan Durbin, Dalton's Parliamentary private secretary, and had to approach Dalton himself more than once before he intervened to require that offers for sale as well as public issues in excess of £50,000 should receive Treasury consent. Today, of course, the consent of the Capital Issues Committee is required for any borrowing of any kind, including from private sources, in excess of £50,000.

The nationalisation of the Bank of England was little more than the formal legislative recognition of an established fact. The clause requiring the clearing banks to obey Treasury directives was more far-reaching in effect, although no sanction is declared in the event of the banks disobeying the directive. This obvious gap in the Act was not mentioned by anybody. It shows, however, that even a Labour Government regards it as unthinkable that the banks would refuse to fall into line with Government policy.

The highlight of the honeymoon year was the passing of the Act nationalising the mines. Miner M.P.s and others marched through the 'Aye' lobby singing songs of victory. Another Labour triumph was the debate in which the sections of the Trades Disputes Act 1927 which were bitterly resented by the trade unions were repealed. Ernest Bevin abandoned for a night the role of Foreign Secretary serving the interests of all sections of the community and made a speech recording his satisfaction that the wrongs of the trade union movement in the General Strike controversy were now being avenged. 'That was the real Bevin', joyfully said dozens of Labour M.P.s, delighted that he was attacking the Tories instead of the Communists.

The American loan presented the Labour Party with its first foretaste of the shape of things to come, but most Labour M.P.s and their supporters, although uneasy about it, regarded it as a matter which concerned the financial experts of the Party rather than themselves. A few months before, the same people had given a tremendous reception to Ernest Bevin when he had declared at Blackpool, 'We stand for bulk purchase.' The acceptance of the American loan was tied up with approval in principle of the Bretton Woods proposals, which were specifically designed to promote international free trade and hence to veto the right of nations to engage in reciprocal bulk purchase or barter. It was a loan which we could not repay on conditions which we could not fulfil. Hugh Dalton was not particularly satisfied with the result of his negotiations and even told me privately that a few votes in protest against the loan could do no harm and might do some good.

The proposals were obviously a blow to the cause of Empire free trade and generally to the conception of Empire development on any terms which would tend to keep the Commonwealth and Empire together. The result of the division was the expected victory for the Government. The odd fact was that while some Labour M.P.s of the so-called right wing—of which I was one—voted against the loan, the two Communist M.P.s and almost all the Communist sympathisers among the ranks of Labour M.P.s voted in favour of it. The whole issue was overshadowed within two years by the acceptance of much larger gifts of money from

C

the Americans under the Marshall plan. The Americans never sought to hold us to the implications of the terms of the loan. But morally they were in a position to say to most left-wing M.P.s, including Crossman and Sydney Silverman, 'You voted for a loan in terms which you had no intention of fulfilling.' Yet it was Sydney Silverman who in 1947 described them as 'shabby moneylenders' to the accompaniment of loud cheers from the Labour M.P.s present.

The honeymoon period lasted a whole year. It was not until the winter of 1946-47 that any serious inroads were made on the popularity of the Labour Government. When the blow fell it had the unfortunate effect of not only exposing appalling incompetence on the part of the Government but of appearing to reflect on the nationalisation of the mines. The general stoppage of industry for three weeks early in 1947 as a result of shortage of coal was entirely unexpected save by a handful of experts. I had been intimately acquainted with the situation because Austins in my constituency were the first big works to be seriously threatened —mainly because they generated a great deal of their own electricity. When Mr Lord announced that he anticipated having to suspend work owing to shortage of coal, there was general incredulity. I telephoned Shinwell, then Minister of Fuel, at his home, and some emergency supplies were rushed to Austins. But these only afforded temporary relief and the anxiety at Austins continued. I had an interview with Shinwell and soon became aware that the stocks of coal were so low that there must be some stoppages in industry in any event. In February the weather turned bitterly cold and the position at Austins became desperate once again. This time, when I again approached the Minister of Fuel and Power, his civil servants had thought of a new method of dealing with me. They said that, although their Ministry was responsible for the production of coal, the allocation of the coal produced was not a matter for them but for the Board of Trade. Off I went to the Board of Trade, who courteously informed me that they exercised only a general supervision over the allocation of fuel to industry but that the Ministry really responsible in this case was the

Ministry of Supply, whose business it was to look after motor manufacturers. The Ministry of Supply, however, said that although they wished to help motor manufacturers, they had no power to allocate coal and I must approach the Ministry of Fuel and Power. It was an unending circle, and even when I explained exactly what was happening to the civil servants concerned in all the Ministries they said that they could do nothing about it. If Government machinery produced unending circles, it was not their fault.

One Friday, later known as Black Friday, I had the adjournment of the House of Commons jointly with the Conservative member for Darwen. I knew already that a very serious announcement was to be made. When Shinwell got up to reply to the debate, I was amazed to hear him spend the first quarter of an hour of his speech on an attack on the Tories for having mismanaged the industry for so long. I was closely watching the faces of the Conservative Members of Parliament opposite and they were showing signs of boredom when Shinwell suddenly and, so far as most of them were concerned, unexpectedly, made the announcement that almost the whole of British industry would have to shut down owing to shortage of coal. To their great credit the Tory members showed no sign whatever of glee at this piece of news which was bound to reflect gravely on Labour in the mind of the floating voter. They looked genuinely aghast at the thought that the country should be so dishonoured in the eyes of the world and should suffer so grievous an injury. Bevan had said, 'This is a country largely made of coal and surrounded by fish. Only an organising genius could produce a shortage of both at the same time.' The organising genius of the so-called planners of the Labour Party had achieved that result within eighteen months.

Oddly enough, some Tory Members of Parliament had warned me not to accept everything I heard from Mr Lord at its face value. They were actuated by jealousy of the attainments of a man immeasurably abler than themselves. They had less excuse for their behaviour than the few ignorant shop stewards who genuinely believed that the industrialists were seeking to sabotage the 'plan' of the

Labour Government. Mr Lord showed his appreciation of the behaviour of the workers at Austins generally by paying wages during the whole of the three weeks the men were out of work due to the miscalculations of Whitehall. Of course, an attempt was made to blame the stoppage on the unusually cold weather, but it can have convinced only the most blinkered Labour supporters.

It was plain to close observers that the much-vaunted Labour plan was no plan at all—even in relation to so vital a factor as stocks of coal about which the Minister of Fuel and Power in Churchill's Government could obtain the most detailed information at two hours' notice at any time from 1940 onwards. Coal and steel are the main factors determining industrial production—and steel depends on coal. A more devastating blow to Labour prestige could not have been dealt as a preliminary to the disasters of 1947. The honeymoon had lasted barely a year. From now onwards Labour had lost room for manoeuvre and before long would condemn itself to the straitjacket of credit squeezes and wage standstills—measures calculated to diminish enterprise and competition and create frustration in the minds of workers as well as business men.

The Minister primarily responsible for the fuel crisis was Shinwell—although he said that he had warned the Cabinet beforehand. As a result, Shinwell was soon dismissed from the Cabinet and made Secretary of State for War. My friend Fred Bellenger was rudely dismissed from that post to make way for him. But before long Shinwell was made Minister of Defence and was spending far more public money on defence than had ever been spent in peace-time before. No doubt from a political standpoint there was something to be said for a left-wing Labour politician to be made to defend huge expenditure on rearmament. But from the point of view of the need to supervise service expenditure, Shinwell's record was hardly likely to arouse confidence. It was he who actually introduced the defence programme which Churchill afterwards admitted to be beyond the capacity of industry to implement—however much money the Treasury under Gaitskell were willing to expend.

CHAPTER VI

The Disillusionment

THE honeymoon period of the Labour Government lasted perhaps a year. By the end of the following year the dissillusionment was complete. Thereafter Labour was able from time to time to present a respectable case for itself on many issues, but it could never hope to recover more than half the lost ground. Indeed, ever since 1947 the political situation has been largely stabilised with minor fluctuations in one direction or the other. Labour never recovered the impetus which it had in 1946. The scenes of enthusiasm which Labour M.P.s and candidates witnessed in 1945 and 1946 vanished—it seems likely, never to return. For at that time the accent was on unity not on disunity, on the forward march not on the correct appraisal of past mistakes. Above all, the totalitarian threat inherent in the attempt or professed attempt to plan the life of a nation was not understood.

Even Communism abroad was regarded as an experiment which had largely justified itself and which must be treated with every outward sign of respect. When Churchill spoke of the 'iron curtain' and of political persecution behind it he was derided. Bevin was considered to be 'pathologically anti-Communist'. One Labour M.P., Norman Dodds, saw what was happening behind the Iron Curtain and told John Freeman and myself of his experiences. When we asked him to speak about it publicly, he exclaimed in horror, 'I could not say anything which could be interpreted as anti-Soviet'. Such was the ideological sympathy for Soviet Communism of men who could not by any stretch of the imagination have been regarded as Communists themselves.

The three factors which completed the disillusionment are not merely of historical interest. They are still present in one form or another in the political scene today. They were, first, the complete failure of Labour's so-called plan (if it ever existed); secondly, Labour's willingness to consider the adoption of outright totalitarianism in the form of direction of labour and its subsequent adoption of repressive and semi-totalitarian measures, namely the credit squeeze, dividend limitation and wage restraint superimposed on the existing edifice of physical controls; thirdly, the revelation that Communism, with which Labour has always had some ideological sympathy as another less democratic form of Socialism, was, when imposed on European peoples, more ruthless and more cruel than Fascism and in many respects more destructive, if less sadistic, than Nazism.

It is difficult to write about Labour's plan because really it never seemed to disclose itself, although a shadowy figure named Sir Edward Plowden was called the chief planner. It is true that exports increased in volume, but with the international scarcities of the post-war period, with Japan and Germany eliminated for the time being as competitors, this was only to be expected. The fuel crisis and the imposition of bread rationing were the most obvious signs of the absence of departmental planning, let alone of the planning of the whole national effort which had been promised at the General Election. Labour had been worried about the measures to be taken to prevent it from being 'tied to the apron-strings of Wall Street'—to use a still current left-wing cliché. In particular, anxieties were expressed lest we should be unable to insulate ourselves from the consequences of an American slump. Today it is considered remarkable when Soviet economists make admissions that Marxist principles do not seem to apply to the post-war American economy. Our domestic Socialist economists have never worn a similar white cloth. Yet with the possible exception of Evan Durbin they have been even more mistaken than is habitual with economists. One would have to be grossly prejudiced or ignorant to deny the outstanding achievements of the so-called capitalist economy of the United States or the very high standard of living enjoyed by American workers. Added to this was the fact manifested from 1947 onwards that it was willing to give away some of its surplus wealth to supposedly advanced countries enjoying the superior benefits of Socialism. In short, the whole Socialist conception that the advantages of competition and free enterprise were illusory and that planning would eliminate work and increase efficiency was falsified by the comparison between post-war America, our benefactor, and post-war Britain, some of whose Socialists delighted in biting the hand that fed them.

Nothing which could be fairly described as a national plan has ever been produced by any Labour Government. Presumably those in authority have been too nervous of the outcome. In this country, whatever its shortcomings, the Civil Service is incorruptible. Figures can be made to appear to prove lies but they cannot be falsified at the source, as in the Soviet Union. Hence if Socialism were ever really enforced in Britain it would be possible to judge of its success, just as it is now possible to make some estimate of the effects of nationalisation on the production of coal and on the efficiency of the railways. I was once rather startled to hear 'Geordie' Buchanan (the only man who refused major political office under Attlee on a point of principle) say to me, 'You know, I no longer believe in nationalisation except, of course, for the public services like coal and transport. The visions we used to have of an ideal form of industrialism under State ownership cannot be realised. Social security has become a fact. Labour will have to find a new dynamic not involving the extension of nationalisation.' Even then this view would not have been deemed as heretical as it sounded. Neither State ownership nor State control are causes which arouse enthusiasm. The best that a Socialist speaker can say to the accompaniment of cheers is something negative in content. 'I am not ashamed to defend nationalisation.' Socialists know that they are on the defensive so far as this subject is concerned. That is why they are so anxious to raise other election issues. That perhaps is why Attlee and Shinwell appointed as first chairman of the Coal Board a great industrialist, Lord Hyndley, whom Aneurin Bevan had mentioned by name at the previous Labour conference as one of those who specialise 'in seeing that one blade of grass will grow where two had grown before'. Ernest Bevin, when asked what he would do about nationalising the chemical industry, answered with similar realistic cynicism: 'Place 'Arry McGowan in charge of it.'

The supreme crisis of Labour occurred during the summer and autumn of 1947 and it was its failure to meet this crisis that determined the political future of the country. The fact that our reserves were bound to be soon exhausted was plain to almost all intelligent observers outside the ranks of Labour. Yet when I made a speech in March, 1947, warning of the coming crisis, I was denounced by Douglas Jay, a leading Socialist economist, on the ground that a relatively slight change in world food prices in our favour would entirely transform the situation. In private conversation he confided that he had his doubts, but at the Party meeting he had been a source of comfort to those who wished to believe that all was well. I noticed afterwards in relation to him as well as others (particularly Crossman, advocate of 'the third force' in the field of foreign affairs) that it did not seem to matter how often or how obviously a so-called expert was proved wrong in his estimates, as long as those estimates were in line with what the Party ideology wished to happen or expected to happen. To a lesser extent the same applied to the Conservative Party. The goodhearted back-benchers of both parties do not mind a man being wrong along Party lines. They mistrusted Churchill as being too clever, yet the really clever politicians who play the Party game consistently, like Butler, McLeod, Boyd-Carpenter, Griffiths, Gaitskell and Callaghan, are regarded as solid and reliable—probably because they can be trusted always to see national issues from a Party standpoint and hence consciously or unconsciously to place the interests of the Party before anything else.

It is now clear that a great dollar crisis was bound to occur whatever happened and that the British economy is permanently precarious due to shortage of gold and dollars. (If South Africa were ever to leave the Commonwealth, our situation would become desperate.) But this fact cannot be held to acquit the Labour Government of the blame for the way in which they reacted to the crisis. At the Labour Party conference which immediately preceded it, no attempt was made to face the issues squarely. Arthur Horner, the Communist miners' leader, warned more clearly of the approaching illness than any Labour leader, although his prescriptions were not realistic.

Soon afterwards I urged in a speech in the House of Commons that the miners should work on Saturdays as the shortage of coal was causing short-time in industry. No Labour M.P. supported me and no Conservative M.P. thought it right to make an appeal which might be so unpopular. It is significant that longer hours of work have never been specifically asked for by any Government, Labour or Conservative, as an answer to the recurring economic crises. In fact—largely due to the work of Ernest Bevin behind the scenes—the miners went back to work on Saturdays and coal production increased very substantially if not proportionately to the increase in hours. But this was an isolated case. The Prime Minister appealed vaguely for harder work, but did not dare to appeal for longer working hours—the one certain way of increasing production. Of course, there were millions of workers who, due to the shortage of steel and coal, would have been unable to work longer hours. But the cause of personal sacrifice in the interests of the country should have been put to the people. I advocated it in my constituency and knew that it would not have been unpopular—so long as the workers had earned more as a result of working longer, as would have undoubtedly occurred. In 1951, when I had become an Independent, I placed on the order paper a motion censuring both the Labour Government and the Conservative Opposition for their failure to advocate the only sure method of increasing production—namely, longer working hours throughout industry on terms to be agreed with the trade union movement. Many members of both sides privately agreed, but none were willing to come out into the open.

When the 1947 financial crisis finally broke, neither the Government nor the Opposition appeared to be ready to meet it. The Opposition voted in the House of Commons

CX

against the Act of Parliament—The Supplies and Services
(Transitional Powers) Act, 1947—which gave the Government a blank cheque to do what they wished with the
persons as well as the property of all British citizens. But the
Conservatives in the House of Lords under the leadership of
Lord Salisbury abstained from voting against the Act which
their leader Churchill had rightly described as outright
totalitarianism. This Act gave the Government power to take
such steps as it wished by regulation to ensure the best use
of the manpower and resources of the nation. As I subsequently forced the Attorney-General to concede, the Bill
gave the Government power to set up concentration camps
as it conferred power to requisition any land and direct
labour to the land so requisitioned. If this power had afterwards been used boldly and ruthlessly instead of timidly and
half-heartedly, it would nevertheless have been granted
without opposition by the Tory peers. Indeed, some Tory
Members of Parliament obviously felt that the totalitarian
powers might be necessary and helpful—provided only that
it was a Tory Government which exercised them. The
supreme crime of the Labour Government in their eyes—but
not in the eyes of their leader Churchill—was its inefficiency,
not its apparent willingness to direct labour.

The meeting of the Parliamentary Labour Party which
preceded the introduction of the 'Dictatorship Bill' was most
instructive. I was convinced from then on that I could not
stay in the Labour Party permanently—unless the views
then expressed were repudiated. Attlee opened the meeting
with a long speech which disclosed no specific plans or
policy. It was primarily an appeal to Party loyalty and an
assurance that it was not to our disadvantage or the advantage of the country for the Tories to return to power and
that therefore the Government should be supported. When
Attlee sat down not more than half a dozen Labour M.P.s
clapped him. In the ensuing debate the point most frequently
made was that Government propaganda was inadequate and
that something must be done about 'spivs'—a term Attlee
said that he had never heard. After a preliminary demonstra-
tion of hostility against my own proposals involving longer

hours of work, I was allowed to elaborate them together with other suggestions for increasing incentive for small employers as well as workers. It was quite clear that if similar proposals had been made by the Government, they would have been supported. But the Government, instead of appealing to the patriotism of the workers and offering them some carrots, chose to show them a big stick which afterwards they never really dared to use.

At this time, if he had responded to suggestions made by many influential people in the ranks of Labour, Bevin might well have been able to supplant Attlee. Confidence in the Prime Minister had never been very great, as Morrison had been the principal author and exponent of Labour's election policy and Bevin undoubtedly the strongest and most-respected person in the Labour movement. Attlee had been regarded as a safe man to whom loyalty was due, but he was not a man to whom people would look for great leadership in an emergency. Bevin could have played this role and would have had wide support outside the ranks of Labour in this country and in America, but his strict sense of loyalty prevented him from entertaining the suggestions made to him. However, he did not expose those engaged in the plot to replace Attlee. One of the ringleaders of the abortive rebellion is today a front-bench Labour trade unionist regarded as a symbol of Party loyalty and orthodoxy. This could hardly have occurred if Bevin had not viewed the project with some sympathy, even though he rejected it.

The introduction of the 'Dictatorship Bill' took place after the Party meeting and immediately before the Houses of Parliament were to adjourn for the summer recess. This is a most significant fact to be borne in mind when the meaning of democracy in Britain is assessed. The Government, it is alleged, has to respond to public opinion as it is expressed by members of Parliament. Yet when the country was told that it faced bankruptcy, Parliament abandoned control over the Government for more than two months after arming that Government with powers similar to those granted to the Governments of Hitler and Mussolini. No specific plans had been produced. Ministers of the Crown had been heard in

virtual silence. The Attorney-General had announced at
two o'clock in the morning that the Government might wish
to direct labour under the Bill. *The Times* had rightly stated
in its leading article that Parliament had given the Government a blank cheque. They had the right to do more or less
what they liked despite the fact that they had told Parliament
that they did not yet know what they wanted to do. Parliament—including the Tories who spoke through the abstention
of the Tory peers in the House of Lords—in effect said,
'We give you the power to go ahead, although we have little
confidence in you.' Incredible as it may seem, the Government in Britain, only two years after the end of the war against
Hitler, had adopted the power to use Hitler's methods. Of
course, they never intended that the powers would be used in
the same way. They would have been willing, at the most, to
adopt the plan which Sir Stafford Cripps believed in—to
create unemployment artificially in the least essential
industries by the withdrawal of essential supplies through
the use of physical controls and thereafter to direct such
unemployed labour into essential industries, such as coal and
steel. On paper this plan would have paid great dividends
for the country. In practice it might well have led to the
imposition of a fully totalitarian régime, if violent opposition
in one form or another had not arisen.

The debates in the House of Commons on the 'Dictatorship
Bill' were unworthy of the causes at stake. Churchill expressed uncompromising and passionate opposition which,
as then a friend of his in private, I knew to be utterly sincere.
The opposition of his colleagues was less outspoken and
more anxious to conciliate the views of a supposed section
of the public that in time of crisis of any kind the Government should be supported where possible and never more
than mildly criticised. This attitude to politics has a super-
ficial attraction. In time of war there is much to be said for
it, although personally I do not believe that the savage
attacks of Aneurin Bevan on Churchill during the war did
anything but good, however far off the mark they often were.
In time of peace, however, the situation is quite different.
Then there is no external enemy against whom it is the duty

of citizens to unite and it becomes monstrous tyranny if they unite against some supposed internal enemy—whether he be stigmatised as a 'spiv' or merely classified as a worker engaged in a non-essential industry.

Just before the debate on the second reading of the Bill I met the Attorney-General, Sir Hartley Shawcross, by accident and expressed my astonishment at the document which was about to be debated. He replied, 'I was very surprised, too, to be telephoned at four o'clock in the morning by the Prime Minister and told to see that a Bill with such wide powers was drafted.' He privately gave me the impression (which I am sure was correct) that wide powers of this nature were not needed. I do not now believe that in drafting and presenting a Bill to Parliament which he himself did not really approve of, he was 'betraying the legal profession'—to use the very words I used to his face about him during the debate—any more than would other members of the legal profession. They are no longer animated, if they ever were, by a passion for personal freedom. They recognise as their twin supreme duties their duty to preserve the outward respectability of the law and their duty to express in legal language or to further by legal means the intentions of their clients. Scientists doubted their professional justification for producing weapons which might destroy the lives of men. Lawyers would have no similar doubts about the drafting of language which would destroy our freedom. Their duty to their clients transcends any other duty—unless it directly conflicts with codes of professional etiquette. If their client is the Government they need have no worry. The Government is the lawful authority in the land whose actions are in law those of the monarch who can do no wrong. The opposition to direction of labour, when it was really threatened, did not come from the lawyers. No law lord raised his voice—let alone a lawyer of note in the country. Direction of labour was halted by means which cannot be accurately assessed but probably chiefly by opposition from the trade union movement. Yet some trade unionists favoured and still favour direction of labour.

In the debate on the Bill, the speech which received the loudest support from the Labour benches was that of Sydney Silverman denouncing the Americans as 'shabby money-lenders' (although he had voted for the American loan). The usually statesmanlike Morrison declined to intervene in the debate to repudiate this suggestion. The most significant speech came from Crossman, the leading intellectual of the Party, who said that the Bill was 'of immense symbolic significance' and added: 'It is not a question of dictatorship. That is inevitable in a modern state.' Although I was nauseated at the time by Crossman's willing acceptance of dictatorship as being inevitable in the modern state, I have since come more and more to agree that his aphorism approximates to the facts—whether there be a Conservative or Labour Government in power. But that does not mean that dictatorship is inevitable. 'The fault, dear Brutus, lies not in our stars, but in ourselves. . . .'

The speech which I made on the second reading of this Bill (against which I was the only Labour member to vote) included the following passage:

'As I see it, the issue is whether or no the assumption by legislative action of totalitarian powers is a substitute for leadership and for vigour in public administration and in public and private enterprise. I claim that in actual fact —and I am sure the Labour Party as a whole agrees with me —the Members of the Labour Party who have spoken in support of the Government today care less for liberty than the aristocrats in 1216 who were responsible for Magna Carta.

'. . . in effect this Bill states that the powers which already exist for the transition period can now be used for peace. . . . As I see it, under this Bill and this subsection, the Government can do anything they like to any person in this nation except throw him into prison. . . . We will be told that it is a temporary measure and only for this emergency. . . . We were told that military conscription was an exceptional measure introduced for two or three years during the emergency. Then . . . the Minister for Defence . . . referred to the introduction of conscription as a normal peace-time measure. Are we here to see the conscription of labour as a normal peace-time measure? It seems to me that this is completely contrary to the whole faith of the Labour Party and that the majority of its members will disagree with it. . . . Was this in our election programme? Have we any mandate for it? On the contrary, we said over and over again that it was our policy at the time of the General Election—and I challenge anyone to deny it—that we stood for a combina-' tion of economic and political democracy; no dragooning and no totalitarianism; and that we stood for increasing the freedom of the individual. That is why I fought the General Election with the Labour Party. . . . There are two kinds of Socialism. There is Totalitarian Socialism in its Communist, Fascist or similar form, and there is liberal, democratic Socialism in which I believe. . . . Hon. Members are betray-ing their election pledges by allowing the Government to have totalitarian powers at this stage. In this issue, let us remember that the pressure seems to come from the so-called "Keep Left" group. . . . But who was the leader of the "Keep Left" movement in the 1929-1931 Government?—Sir Oswald Mosley. I claim that the best friends of the Labour Party are not the people attempting to utilise this situation to produce this, that or the other measure which they are trying to impose in a hurry on the Government, but those who stand by the election policy of the Labour Government. I believe the central issue was put two thousand years ago, when the Jews tried to make Jesus of Nazareth accept the view that He was going to stand against Roman tyranny. They asked whether it was lawful that they should pay tribute unto Caesar. He told them to bring Him a penny and then asked whose image, whose superscription, was on it. They said "Caesar's", and He said, "Render unto Caesar the things that are Caesar's and unto God the things that are God's." It is the tragedy of totalitarian governments that they render unto Caesar the things that are God's.'

I had a great deal of trouble with my constituency Party which held two private meetings by way of inquest. They ended with a unanimous vote of confidence—to the surprise of many people. When the vote finally came on direction of

labour, five Labour M.P.s voted against it and nearly a
hundred managed to absent themselves for one reason or
another, and so in effect to abstain. A handful of people
were directed under the Control of Engagements Order,
but very considerable numbers must have been 'persuaded'
by the threat of direction of labour to go from one employment to another or from one area to another. Nevertheless,
direction of labour was never really introduced and anyone
with sufficient determination or guile could have circum-
vented it.

That this was so I soon came to realise as a result of a
letter from a Welshman. He apparently had religious reasons
for conscientious objection to joining a trade union. The
mines are a 'closed shop'. He enquired whether in such
circumstances he could or would be directed to work in the
mines. My secretary, Mrs Shirley, a lady of great ability as
well as charm, sent the letter to the Minister of Labour and
received a reply from his secretary that no man with a
conscientious objection to trade unions would be directed
into any employment in which a closed shop existed. This, of
course, disclosed that the plans of the Government to direct
people into essential industry could be easily frustrated—as
there is a closed shop throughout essential industry. Mrs
Shirley, having shown me what she had done, gave the
letter to the Press with the result that it was treated as a
statement of Government policy. She had specifically confirmed beforehand that the Minister stood by the letter and
knew it would be publicised. Shortly afterwards Churchill
saw me by chance in the corridor and congratulated me on
the shrewdness of a manoeuvre for which I failed to inform
him that my secretary was solely responsible.

The financial crisis which led to the introduction of
direction of labour was, of course, solved by the grant of
'Marshall Aid'. Being at the time a friend of the American
Ambassador, I knew what was in the wind and how much
was due to American admiration for Ernest Bevin, who after
Marshall himself was the main architect of the European
Recovery Programme. Lewis Douglas told me privately
that it was his determination (in which characteristically

Churchill himself concurred) that no one in these islands should ever be able to say that America had refused to help us because we had a Socialist Government in power. Of course, a Communist or an extreme Socialist would say that this intention may have been genuine but only because Bevin and his colleagues were not really Socialists. At that time, however, Labour, having more or less completed the nationalisation of fuel and transport, appeared to be about to nationalise steel. No opposition of any kind to the nationalisation of steel was ever expressed by the American Secretary of State.

CHAPTER VII

Foreign Affairs

DURING these two years—the honeymoon year and the
year of disillusionment—I had from time to time been
drinking heavily. But I did not allow drink to interfere
seriously with my work. For instance, when the 'Dictatorship
Bill' came before the House, I decided to make several
speeches, fighting it all the way. As the House sat all through
the night this involved a considerable strain. But Churchill
had told me that if I intended to fight I should speak
whenever I could manage to get myself called. During this
long night I had nothing at all to drink. I must have already
sensed the danger of drink, although I should have regarded
it as ridiculous if anyone had made the suggestion that I was
a potential alcoholic.

From 1945 onwards I was obsessed by the problems presented to this country and the world by the atomic bomb.
Immediately after the atomic bomb was dropped at Hiroshima, I made an intensive study of the principles of nuclear
physics although I have no natural bent for science. In
Parliament I became acting Chairman of the Committee of
members of both Houses and of distinguished scientists who
studied the political implications of atomic energy. I also
became joint Honorary Secretary and later Deputy Chairman of the Parliamentary and Scientific Committee.

I believe that my intense preoccupation with this subject
played a significant, if small, part in causing my slow but
sure descent into alcoholism. It is, of course, typical of the
alcoholic to find excuses for drinking both before and after
the event and this may be just one more example of the
tendency. Certainly the sad story of the failure of the nations
of the world to accept an effective system of international
control of atomic energy did not provide a conscious excuse

for drinking. But rightly or wrongly, I believe it was a factor that contributed in some degree to create the mental background which impelled me towards alcoholism. I began to feel that modern industrial civilisation might well be a disease in process of working out its own destruction by means of its own creation. It seemed self-evident that unless international control of atomic energy could be established, the future for civilised man would be precarious. Once the Soviet Union possessed atomic bombs, I argued, it would be most unlikely that a final settlement could be achieved. The West would then be no longer in a position to negotiate from strength. Time was not on our side, as Attlee and Bevin seemed to imagine. I came to the conclusion that a settlement must be achieved before the Soviet Union developed atomic bombs—and although almost every Western scientist prophesied that this could not be before about 1955, I had openly expressed grave doubts about their prophecies. I had found Professor Oliphant a very reliable guide and he had always warned me that the Soviet Union might confound everyone with the speed at which their programme would progress. As the years went by and the prospect of any settlement with the Soviet Union receded, the background of my mind became gloomier and gloomier. This had more effect on me than the manifest failures of what some people called British Socialism.

Within a few weeks of being elected to Parliament I became a crucial if minor figure in an event of great importance. I had approached a number of scientists and been helped by them to understand not only their point of view on the political implications of the new discoveries in nuclear physics but the principles on which the development of atomic energy depended. One day I was sent to see a certain individual whose name I am glad to say I have never disclosed, drunk or sober, to anyone. He read to me excerpts from the top secret agreement which had been reached between Churchill and Roosevelt at Quebec about the atomic bomb (then a project) and the development of atomic energy (already an accomplished fact). This top-secret agreement was never disclosed by Churchill to his

Cabinet and had not been disclosed by Attlee to his Cabinet. The agreement provided that the consent of the Prime Minister of Britain should be obtained before the President of the United States of America authorised the use of the atomic bomb in action. But it also left the peaceful development of atomic energy in Britain as well as America largely subject to the discretion of the President of the United States.

Certain leading British scientists who knew of the agreement felt that it greatly hampered the British atomic effort. They wished this country to be free to pursue its own programme without the necessity of consulting and obtaining the consent of the United States. I was advised that the most likely method of redressing the situation was for an obvious leakage of the fact to be made in the House of Commons. I accordingly made a disclosure about the secret agreement in an adjournment debate in November, 1945, to which Herbert Morrison was to reply. Morrison himself was most startled and was obviously not fully aware of the agreement—so great secrecy still surrounded the whole subject. Dalton, whom I accompanied later to his room, clearly knew even less about it than Morrison. Just as before the bomb was dropped Churchill had kept its very existence a secret from the Cabinet, so Attlee kept the agreements governing atomic energy a secret after the surrender of Japan—and with far less justification. That night, as I walked out of the Chamber, Bevin said to me, 'I will see you in the morning. I know the two men who told you about this agreement—there can be only two. Your speech will mean that they will go to penal servitude and I regret I can't get it done to you as well.'

As a result of my speech President Truman was questioned at length the next day and refused to accept my statements (which, of course, have since been proved correct by the publication of the agreement). He said that broadly speaking America and Britain were 'in equal partnership over the production of the bomb'. This was not in fact so, but it was obviously most helpful to Britain that he should have said so. A few days later, Churchill, after saying in relation to my speech that an obvious leakage had occurred, said that

President Truman's observations clearly provided an excellent starting-point for further negotiations. In fact, my advisers had proved right, and the leakage, by exposing the unfairness of the clause leaving British developments in some circumstances subject to the discretion of the American President, had given Attlee a very strong card to play. Evidently the American President was not willing to insist on any interpretation of the clause which would restrict the rights of Britain as an equal partner. In the result, Attlee bargained away the British right to consultation over the use of the bomb in exchange for the right for Britain to go ahead with its atomic programme without consulting the U.S.A. But that did not emerge for many years. It is quite clear that if there had been full publication of the Quebec Agreement and Attlee had been a powerful enough negotiator, we would have come to far more satisfactory terms with America and our co-operation with the American project would have continued to the advantage of both sides. The lesson to be learned from these events is that while it may be right that diplomatic negotiations should take place in secret, the agreements that are concluded should be made public, and that whereas such agreements may be kept secret for security reasons in wartime, they should be disclosed as soon as possible after the war is finished.

Bevin sent for me the day after my speech and said, ' "X" told you about this agreement. You can help undo the terrible damage you have done by signing a statement against him immediately.' I refused and indeed denied that I had received any secret information. (I regarded this as a white lie.) He then mentioned another distinguished person—'Y'— and tried to get me to make a statement against him. Both 'X' and 'Y' are today in positions of even greater importance than they then held. Bevin disclosed that he knew that I had met 'X' on three occasions. It is obvious, therefore, that either 'X' or myself or both were being shadowed. No possible suggestion of Communist sympathies could have been made against any of us. Although technically I may have been in the wrong over all this, I was convinced that I was morally in the right. Long afterwards many exalted persons acknowledged that it was one of the few occasions when such a leakage was justified.

Partly because of this disclosure and partly because I took the adjournment of the House of Commons time after time on the subject of control of atomic energy, I became regarded as an expert on it and was even described in the Bulletin of the Atomic Scientists of Chicago (where the first atomic pile was built) as 'the conscience of the House of Commons on atomic energy'. I visited Harvard, Yale, Columbia and Chicago Universities on behalf of the Committee on Atomic Energy set up by the New Commonwealth of which Churchill was President. The Baruch Commission which represented the U.S.A. at the United Nations impressed me greatly. Their knowledge of the subject was exhaustive and I felt that they were determined to obtain an agreement for the international control of atomic energy, if in any way it were possible. When I asked at luncheon, 'What steps should the West take if the Soviet Union will not co-operate?', I was answered, 'We are not prepared to consider any such eventuality. Our task is to secure agreement. We are forbidden to consider the possibility or the consequences of failure.'

Of course, great efforts were made by Communists to exploit the natural repugnance which scientists felt at the use to which their labours had been put. At a private meeting of the American Federation of Scientists, I participated in a discussion as to whether they should be affiliated to a world organisation of scientists of which Professor Joliot-Curie (who was present) would be President and Professor Bernal and a Russian professor Vice-Presidents. Dr Szilard, the Chicago professor who headed the team which first produced an atomic chain reaction in 1942, quietly asked, 'We know that our distinguished colleague Professor Joliot-Curie is a Communist, as is Professor Bernal. May we have a similar assurance regarding the Russian professor?' Even so, the proposal that the American Federation of Scientists should be affiliated to a Communist-front organisation was only narrowly defeated. At the time the American Federation of Scientists was immensely important, representing the majority of the scientists who had been responsible for the atomic bomb. They educated American public opinion on the facts concerning atomic energy to an extent far greater than was ever achieved in Britain. Indeed, at this meeting Dr Robert J. Oppenheimer, the scientist who had been in charge of Los Alomos where the bomb itself was made, said, 'Our propaganda has been so effective that it is in danger of leading misguided persons to advocate a preventive war against the Soviet Union if they will not accept inspection of their territory for the control of atomic energy.'

The high-water mark of such efforts as were made to achieve international control of atomic energy was reached when the Sub-Committee of scientists at the United Nations including the representatives of the Soviet Union signed a report in 1948 showing that control of atomic energy was feasible through a system of international inspection. Alas, it has long since ceased to be feasible. This is because the essential elements for the production of atomic weapons, namely uranium and thorium, have by now become so widely distributed that substantial quantities could easily be concealed; also because very important new developments have taken place which make it easier to produce fissionable material. But at this time, when it was feasible, the political representative of Stalin maintained that aerial inspection was incompatible with national sovereignty. I believed that an attempt should be made to break the deadlock by means of a high-level meeting between the heads of state. Year after year I put down a motion on the order paper advocating such a meeting. I was supported by Clement Davies, leader of the Liberal Party, by Arthur Salter and by several Labour M.P.s. At a special broadcast at a peak hour arranged at my request by Sir William Haley, the proposal was discussed and supported by Bertrand Russell, by Professor P. M. S. Blackett, and by General Sir Frederick Morgan, who was soon to be given a supreme post in the British atomic effort. Churchill privately agreed and publicly made the same proposal as part of his election platform in 1950. I am sure that much earlier an overwhelming majority of the British people would have favoured a summit meeting. But the proposal (which was never debated in Parliament except in the course of debates initiated by myself as a private member) was blocked by the paramount authority of Ernest Bevin. He had set his face resolutely against anything in the nature of a summit meeting and Attlee was completely under his domination.

Bevin was indeed the most powerful figure in British politics in the years after the war. He was a vulgar man, grossly illiterate but possessed of great genius and massive strength. He was by far the most egotistical person I have ever met. But it was a form of egotism which commanded respect and even affection. He would sit in the luncheon room surrounded by his cronies listening to his interminable and boring stories about Bob Smillie, Ben Tillett and other trade union leaders of his earlier years. These occasions reminded me of army messes where if the Colonel tells a weak story everyone laughs uproariously. One day I ventured to put a word in about the fact that I had recently read all the books available in the library about Stalin. I was about to make some comment which I regarded as appropriate when Bevin exclaimed with vehemence, 'Stalin, 'e don't count!' This ended the matter. Yet on other occasions he would speak about Stalin with great understanding and shrewdness. Above all, he was interested in economic affairs and particularly in Professor Vargas who had written articles showing that the modern capitalist world did not necessarily always behave as foretold in the doctrines of orthodox Marxism. His exclamation, 'Stalin, 'e don't count', was not intended as a snub for me (although he had a dislike for all those whom he might label as 'intellectuals'). It was an emotional outburst emanating from his deep confidence in the vast resources of the free world as against what he believed to be the apparent but brittle strength of Communism. It always appeared to me that he tended to underestimate his opponents. In debate he very rarely answered his political enemies—particularly those in his own party. He used to annihilate them with some irrelevant aside showing both his sense of humour and his contempt for them. Some indeed of his speeches were almost unintelligible.

He remains a great man despite all his faults. He was intensely loyal. He would listen to no talk of his supplanting Attlee to whom he had given his loyalty. In 1944 Laski said to Bevin, 'I am convinced that Attlee has not got the stature to be a Labour Prime Minister. I am equally sure that Herbert Morrison has the stature, but the trade unions will not have him. You are the only other man for the job and if you are willing to go for it I will support you and so will many of my friends.' Bevin refused indignantly. Two years afterwards, when I made some remark about Laski who was a very generous and honourable man, Bevin said, ' 'E's an intriguer. 'E wanted me to put up for Prime Minister. I knew that like other Jews 'e wanted to make me 'is Messiah only to crucify me afterwards.'

This deep-rooted loyalty he felt not only for his leader, whether it was Churchill or Attlee, but for his trade union, his Party and his country. When the great depression of 1931 came and Macdonald deserted the Labour Party, Bevin was a tower of strength. He helped immensely to build up the financial resources of his own union and thereby to ensure that if another General Strike ever took place the workers would not be the losers. It was he who struck a deadly blow at the beloved George Lansbury, whose pacifist principles were endangering not only his own Party's future but his country's safety. It is indeed odd that the friend of Lenin should have been a pacifist. By attacking Lansbury Bevin paved the way for Attlee to become Prime Minister, as the Parliamentary Party could not choose between Morrison and Greenwood. Indeed, both on and off stage Bevin played over many years a part of crucial importance in the national life.

Great as had been his work as Minister of Labour in the war, he performed his greatest service to his country and the world in the three or four years that followed it. No one but Ernest Bevin could have mobilised the Labour and trade union movements into opposition to Communism at that time. Indeed, it is almost certainly true to say that for two or three years a majority of the rank and file of his own Party thought him to be pathologically anti-Communist and believed that he was not pursuing a Socialist foreign policy

(whatever that may mean). But so great was their respect
for the man, and, in the last resort, for his judgment that
time and again he routed his critics and triumphed with
effortless ease. Somehow, whatever they might say, they felt
that Ernie could not be wrong. He knew how to play on the
emotions of a Labour Party Conference with consummate
artistry. Yet one even wondered whether it was artistry or
merely that the man's mind was naturally attuned to his
audience. Somehow it was impossible to think of Ernest Bevin
as a man who deliberately planned his effects.

Bevin was immensely respected in Europe. But more
important for the future of the Labour Party was his reputation in America. Without the Marshall Plan, as even
Aneurin Bevan admitted, there would have been two million
unemployed, at least. Bevin deserves the main credit, so far
as Britain is concerned, for the thousands of millions of
dollars that were given to Europe by a country which might
quite easily have regarded Europe as their competitor in the
markets of the world. Workers in automobile factories in
America paid increased taxes to help Britain keep up an
export trade in cars which might have put them out of work.
This was a triumph for Bevin, whose foreign policy was
bitterly attacked by men who had done little for the Labour
Party or their own country.

Throughout this vital period after the war, when Bevin
rarely obtained a cheer from the Labour benches because,
knowing the realities of Communism, he knew that we must
ally ourselves with America and that the projected 'third
force' would prove to be the last weakness, he preserved a
great sense of judgment. At a moment crucial for his own
popularity he moved the Trades Disputes Act 1946 which
removed from the Statute Book the clauses of the 1927 Act
so hated by trade unionists. About the same time he made a
speech on foreign policy which commanded support from
the Labour Party as well as the Tories. In the course of it he
said that he was willing to sit down with the Foreign
Secretary of any country in the world for the purpose of
devising a franchise for a directly-elected government of the
peoples of the world. This speech has since been the sheet-

anchor of a world-wide movement for World Government. At the time I felt sure that it was intended to appeal to the idealist section of the Labour Party and help to compensate in their woolly minds for his realistic attitude towards the Soviet Union.

This, however, was not so. After the speech, made on a Friday, I was in the Strangers' Bar with William Barkley of the *Daily Express* and Percy Cater of the *Daily Mail*. Neither of them regarded the speech as remarkable and Barkley said he could not understand it. Ernest Bevin waddled into the Bar and, although unpopular with him at the time, I offered him a drink which he accepted. He then placed himself between Barkley and Cater. Bevin asked what they thought of the speech. Barkley, who fears neither God nor man and Lord Beaverbrook only a little, replied without an instant's hesitation that he could not understand what it was all about. This was the only occasion on which I ever saw the slightest sign of a puncture in Bevin's monolithic self-assurance. But within a moment he dictated to Barkley and Cater the exact words he had used about world government and added, 'They'll be reading those words in the 'istory books in a 'undred years' time from now.'

A few months later I visited Harvard University and was allowed to meet Professor J. B. Conant, who had been Chairman of the Committee which advised Presidents Roosevelt and Truman on atomic energy. Before very long I had to make way for an American senator, but as Conant shook my hand he said, 'Were you present on that occasion when your Foreign Secretary, Mr Bevin, said that he was willing to sit down with the Foreign Secretary of any country in the world for the purpose of devising a franchise for a directly-elected government of the peoples of the world?' I said, 'Yes, sir.' He went on, 'Do you know that I often say that that speech will be read in the history-books in a hundred years' time from now?' On returning to England I told this to Bevin. He replied, 'Of course.'

But although Bevin was egotistical, he was devoid of personal ambition, at any rate in the political sense. Although he was capable of grave indiscretions he was capable of a

very high standard of diplomacy, particularly in his dealings
with the Americans who became his firm friends in spite of
his domestic politics. That he failed with the Soviet Union
can hardly be blamed on him. He had pledged the Labour
Government to have 'the cards on the table face upwards'.
He had inherited the Teheran and Yalta agreements in
which, as we now see, Churchill was overborne by Roosevelt
to agree to many clauses which were bound to be regarded
by the Soviet Union as surrenders to their point of view. Yet,
not so long after, Bevin helped to save Persia from Soviet
domination by insisting on a public reference of the Persian
complaint against the Soviet Union to the United Nations.
His record over Greece during the period when most of the
world (including most Americans) were denouncing the
British as imperialists for helping to save Greece from
Communism, was excellent. His name came to count throughout Europe in circles far removed from Royal Palaces or
Foreign Embassies. The humble farm labourer's son from
Winsford had become one of the most powerful figures on
the world scene without losing his early sense of loyalty to
the underdog.

His personal relationships were, with some notable exceptions as with Churchill, Attlee and most trade union leaders,
not perhaps his strongest point. He had violent personal
dislikes. The most important was of Herbert Morrison.
Towards the end of his life there was some slight modification
in his attitude to Morrison, partly because he could not fail
to recognise that Morrison had helped to defeat his own
most bitter enemies in the Labour Party. But this antagonism
had done the Labour Party little good. Equally strong was his
dislike of Lord Beaverbrook. On one of the two occasions on
which he gave me interviews as Forces Editor of *Reynolds
News* on demobilisation, he asked me to refer to Lord
Beaverbrook as 'The Minister of Chaos'. This was a reference
to some current joke or dispute among higher level Ministers
or civil servants—I never discovered which—but it was
intended to be a personal affront. Beaverbrook as a journalist
would be bound to know that at the time the *Reynolds News*
correspondent would be a reflection of Bevin, particularly as

I was then allowed to quote him. That Beaverbrook was dismissed in the war by his close friend Winston Churchill (whose adviser he continued to be) must be attributed in a large degree to Bevin. It seemed to me extraordinary that so great a man as Bevin should wish to have a petty jibe poked at a former colleague who, whatever his faults, had undoubtedly helped to produce the fighters and bombers in 1940.

Bevin rapidly became a great favourite with Foreign Office officials. He soon regarded them as members of another trade union over which he presided. By so doing, he commanded their loyalty but he probably went much too far. Official files, particularly top secret files, look very impressive. They are immaculately presented in surroundings of great pomp and dignity but whether they really represent the vital facts is another question. It is all too easy for a very busy man to read a memorandum and approve it and then adopt part of it in the brief of the speech he is about to make. From what I have seen and heard I should imagine that there was only one man in our time capable of keeping the Civil Service really on their toes, capable on his own of exposing inaccuracies and weaknesses in an official report or brief—and that, of course, was Winston Churchill. (Oddly enough, there is some evidence that on departmental matters this applied in a minor degree to Aneurin Bevan, despite his enormous over-expenditure on the Health Service at its beginning.)

When Bevin died I had ceased to be a member of the Labour Party. I made a few enquiries to find out whether the Government proposed to have him buried in Westminster Abbey. Clearly nothing was being done about it. So I put down a direct question to the Prime Minister for oral answer, asking him whether he would make arrangements for Ernest Bevin to be buried in Westminster Abbey. Attlee replied tartly and misleadingly, 'The wishes of his widow should be considered in this matter.' A few members murmured approval.

I had been sitting downstairs drinking with Arthur Greenwood and I immediately reported to him what had happened. 'Nonsense', he said. 'I am sure Mrs Bevin would be proud to have Ernie buried in the Abbey. Get Will Glenvil Hall and Clem. Davies to approve a letter from you to her and then get your friend Winston to initial it as well. Then the Government cannot prevent it.' I went straight to Glenvil Hall and Davies and they both approved immediately. So did Churchill. I handed the letter to William Whiteley, the Chief Whip, who said that he would deal with the matter and get the Prime Minister to speak to Mrs Bevin himself. This took only about thirty minutes and could easily have been done by any of the leading Government members whom I had asked about it more than once.

Some people have cavilled at the idea that the remains of such a man should lie in Westminster Abbey, but if the roll were called of all those buried there, the name of Ernest Bevin would stand high in the eyes of all who respect determination, outspokenness and service to one's fellow men.

CHAPTER VIII

Churchill

By far the most important influence in my political life was Winston Churchill. My friendship with him was of my own seeking. On the very first day when Parliament met I waited in the lobby outside the House and asked Eden to let me have a few words with him. I told him that whatever the result of the election might have been, the British people as a whole, including those who had voted against him, felt the same about him personally as they had thought in the worst days of the war.

I cannot remember how or when it came about that he first invited me to his home at Chartwell. But from the autumn of 1946 until 1951 I saw him from time to time at Chartwell or sometimes in his room at the House of Commons. He expressly told me that I could see him or speak to him on the telephone whenever I wished and must have given instructions to that effect to his secretaries. I did not avail myself of this privilege unless I felt that I had something of value to say. It is one of the best traditions of the House that friendships can be formed between men of different political parties. There was nothing dishonourable in Churchill having admitted me on some matters to his confidence, although I was a member of the Labour Party. Never did he ask me to do or say anything against my Party. It was only when I had already decided to take a particular line— as on the issue of direction of labour—that he gave me advice. When finally I left the Labour Party I did so entirely on my own decision without any prompting from him, and obviously knowing my weakness he told me to be very careful in my personal behaviour from then on, as I should be closely watched by hostile eyes. He even asked me to become teetotal for six months. I agreed, but I did not keep my agreement. The next time I met him he offered me a whisky and soda and I accepted. I have often wondered whether he did this to test me. If so, I was found wanting.

I always believed and still believe that Winston Churchill is the greatest Englishman since William Shakespeare. He does not agree with this assessment of his place in history. I know, because I once inscribed a humble work of my own with the words: 'To the greatest Englishman since William Shakespeare', and while placing the volume in a special bookcase (from which, no doubt, it has long been removed) Mr Churchill said that the inscription was 'not apt'. This remark was no false modesty. That vice which blooms as a supposed virtue in the rich soil of English hypocrisy has no place in the mind or the heart of the man whose ruthless benignity helped to save the cause of freedom.

Some laborious gentleman once wrote that genius is an infinite capacity for taking pains. Certainly Mr Churchill possesses that quality, but so to circumscribe his genius would be an insult to it. His genius rather consists in a quite extraordinary array of talents ranging from intense powers of concentration to a childish sense of fun, from implacable hatred of the enemy to an affection for him as soon as the fray is over. He himself selected 'content of thought' as the most important attribute in speaking. That is why his speeches, almost always delivered with great eloquence and capable of arousing deep emotion, were even better when read the next day. The jokes did not sparkle so brightly, but the underlying purpose and effect were clearer. From his earliest years he took immense trouble over his speeches. Even during the period when I knew him well, from 1947 to 1951, he would correct and recorrect his books and speeches, keeping four secretaries busy at all times of the day and night and even using a magnificent phonograph as well.

He is a small but stockily built man. That he possesses great physical as well as moral courage can be told at a glance at the face which is known so well. Often the stern expression is replaced by the impish but innocent look of a chubby child. Baldwin once quoted Cardinal Newman in welcoming Churchill back to the House of Commons after an illness at the time when Churchill was attacking the National Government:

'And in the morn those angel faces smile
Which we have loved long since and lost awhile.'

It has always seemed to me that the background of his mind is imbued with a sense of chivalry now rarely encountered in the modern world. I remember one day in his study at Chartwell when he asked me some question about Aneurin Bevan. Suddenly he became enraged and charged up and down the room, head lowered like a bullock. 'I could wish for a revival of the manners of ancient times. I would challenge him to a duel.' The duel would have had to take place with pistols as Churchill's right arm is partially paralysed as a result of a wound suffered in a cavalry charge long before Aneurin Bevan was born. Yet when Bevan makes a speech of which Churchill approves—as occasionally happens—he is willing to recognise its merit. Churchill's intermittent outbursts of fury against Socialists are not basically due to overweening love of the Tories, whom he largely blames for what he calls the unnecessary war. These outbursts are due to a deep-rooted anger at the thought that anyone in these islands should not give first place in his heart to the cause of the British Commonwealth and Empire.

That indeed has been the main theme and purpose of his long life—to enhance the power and the glory of the British Commonwealth and Empire. This description of the many countries owing allegiance to the Crown was first used by Churchill himself who was brought up in the Victorian era when the British Empire was at the height of its power. It is not true to say that Churchill feared self-government for native peoples if he felt that they were ready for it. What he really feared was severance of these peoples from the family circle over which the mother country presides. I saw this on the day when Attlee announced in the House of Commons the settlement negotiated in India under which it appeared that neither India nor Pakistan would leave the Commonwealth. It is the practice for the Leader of the Opposition to

D

be given an advance copy of any important statement to be made in Parliament. I had been invited to lunch at Churchill's country house at Chartwell, and was sitting in the garden with him when the message arrived. After he had read it, he passed it over to me. The safeguards against immediate chaos and ultimate totalitarianism seemed to me inadequate, and confidently expecting that he would agree, I said so. His mind, however, was made up in the other direction. During lunch he reverted to the topic and pointed out advantages in the proposed method of leaving India. Finally I said, 'Sir, if you really feel that, surely you should pay tribute to the Government?' Churchill frowned and I felt that the conscious-ness of the moral correctness of my attitude was hardly sufficient to compensate me for the tacit rebuke. When Attlee announced the settlement that afternoon, Churchill made a reasoned and cautious statement, but he ended with words of hope. 'If events should proceed for the best', he said, 'it would reflect great credit on Earl Mountbatten and', he added almost as he resumed his seat, 'on the Prime Minister who appointed him.' There was hardly a cheer from the packed Tory benches. But Churchill's relief at the prospect that India might not leave the Commonwealth outweighed everything else in his mind.

For the cause of Britain and the Commonwealth he would be ruthless as well as magnanimous. I am certain that if Hitler had invaded in 1940 he would have gone to any lengths to prevent defeat. The King would undoubtedly have been advised to leave these shores for the New World in the sure faith that the New World 'would rise to the rescue and liberation of the old'. Much against his own wishes, he surely would have been bound to follow the advice of his Prime Minister. Churchill told me that if the worst had come to the worst he would have gone into the hills to fight it out. Of the two persons he would have taken with him, he mentioned one, Ernest Bevin. He had always the most tremendous admiration and affection for this gifted, more obstinate, more egotistical but equally massive counterpart of himself. There can be little doubt that the other would have been Anthony Eden, who although quite unlike

Churchill in character is regarded with great affection as well as respect by him. One day when my father, who is a doctor, told Churchill that if he continued to drink wine and smoke cigars he would live to be a hundred, Churchill answered, 'Pray do not tell that to Anthony.' It was an impish joke, for Churchill was convinced that the causes in which he believed would be safer in the hands of Eden than of anyone except himself.

The ruthlessness of Churchill in defence of the Common-wealth was shown above all in his attitude to the Soviet Union. He hated Communism from the depths of his heart. He was not reconciled to it because Stalin toasted him in the presence of Roosevelt as the man who more than any other had ensured the final victory in the war. He hated it. But because it was a fact, he acknowledged it. He even compromised with it. 'Do you not think', he once said to me, 'that I did not know when I shook the hand of Stalin that I was shaking the hand of a murderer?' He had written of the Soviet Union in the course of an essay on Shaw: 'This is a land where man, sunk in the depths of a world's miseries, is even denied the hope of a better life in a world to come.' Yet he became the chief external protagonist of the Soviet Union in the hour of its mortal peril.

Such was his ruthless determination to save Britain and the cause of freedom. He even advised Vernon Bartlett to soft-pedal any exposure of the grim reality of life in the Soviet Union. But he would not have compromised for any other cause—not even to save a hero. I always sus-pected this, but it was proved to me in the following circumstances.

In early 1947 I visited Paris for a private interview with Kimon Georgiev, then the Foreign Secretary of Bulgaria. He had been leader of the Fatherland Front and Prime Minister. When I asked him whether the supporters of Nilola Petkov, the leader of the Parliamentary Opposition were being beaten up by the Communists, he replied, 'Why, my own supporters are being beaten up by them all the time.' Georgiev, who is a very astute and brave man, while appearing to work with the Communists did everything in his power to save his friends. He sent to Britain, as Minister, Professor Dolaptchieff, to whom I was introduced by my friend Michael Padev. I was constantly briefed by him about Bulgarian affairs. Finally Petkov was arrested and placed on trial. He defended himself with great courage. The trial and subsequent execution of Petkov clearly showed that the Soviet Union intended to rule the countries behind the Iron Curtain with absolute ruthlessness and leave them with not even the semblance of independence.

Two or three days before Petkov was hanged—an unpleasant process lasting some ten minutes in Bulgaria—I received an urgent message to see the Bulgarian Minister. On arriving at the Bulgarian Legation I could tell immediately from his grave appearance that he was suffering a personal tragedy. He did not say, but I knew that he would resign his post as Minister and remain an exile from his native country if the judicial murder of Petkov took place. He told me that he had heard from Georgiev that Petkov would be executed within a very short time. One could hardly believe that so hideous a crime would be perpetrated even by the quislings of Bulgaria. Petkov had been a leader of the Resistance Movement in Bulgaria and Deputy Prime Minister in the post-war Government. The Nazis had treated him roughly but they had not hanged him. Could it be that the Communists would do what even the Fascists would not do?

Dolaptchieff said that any further approach from our Foreign Office, even by Ernest Bevin himself, could not hope to have any effect. The decision was taken, not in Sofia but in Moscow. The Bulgarian Government did what they were told by their Russian masters. According to his information it was Stalin himself who had taken the decision. Only by Stalin himself could the decision be reversed. Stalin would take no notice of a message from Ernest Bevin, much less from Clement Attlee. The only hope would be a personal appeal or message from Winston Churchill who, although out of office, had greater prestige behind the Iron Curtain than any man outside it. Dolaptchieff would not guarantee that a message from Churchill would save Petkov's life,

but he believed it quite possible that it would. Time was very
short and if a message were to go, it must go now.

The Bulgarian Legation contained, of course, a number of
Communists who spied on Dolaptchieff. Fortunately he was
able to put a private telephone at my disposal. I proceeded
to telephone Mr Churchill at Chartwell in the presence of
the Professor, his wife and Michael Padev. I put Mr Churchill
in possession of the facts and said, 'I am not asking you to
send a message. I would not dare, sir, to do more than let
you know what the Minister himself says, who is with me
now, and then ask for your decision.' There was scarcely a
pause before the the resonant voice replied, 'I will send the
following cable, if you want, to Stalin: "If Petkov dies I will
denounce you for the foul murderer that you are".' This
telegram Professor Dolaptchieff did not wish to be sent.
Three days later Petkov died and Dolaptchieff resigned his
post as Minister. He now works in the Overseas Service of
the B.B.C.

The incident shows that Winston Churchill was not willing
to adopt any attitude other than defiance to save the life of a
hero. Yet Churchill has always believed almost with passion
in high-level conversations with heads of states. There can
be no doubt that he achieved more than anyone else in his
direct talks with Stalin and that President Roosevelt's
contribution, particularly at Yalta, was unfortunate to say
the least. Churchill and Stalin respected one another as
realists. During the war there were many occasions when
Stalin made himself inaccessible to foreign ambassadors.
Churchill devised a method of enabling Sir Archibald Clark
Kerr (afterwards Lord Inverchapel) to see Stalin. He gave
Clark-Kerr a letter marked 'Strictly Personal' to Stalin,
with instructions that it should be handed over by Clark-
Kerr in person. As a result Clark-Kerr not only saw Stalin,
but was able to establish a personal relationship with him so
close that he was always able to see him thereafter except at
the worst stage of the British-Soviet dispute over Poland.

Churchill broods long over his favourite problems in
international affairs. He has the immense advantage of a
lifetime of almost unexampled experience in them. Ernest

Bevin used to say that the greatest danger of war arose in the
Middle East. There can be few people whose knowledge of
the Middle East can rival Churchill's. He fought in Egypt
and the Sudan as a young subaltern. He was sponsor for the
Balfour Declaration. (Weizmann told me that although
Labour is traditionally pro-Israel, he would prefer Churchill
to any leader of the Socialists.) Lawrence of Arabia worked
under Churchill after the First World War and Churchill
was largely responsible for the post-war settlement in the
Middle East. Well might he say to the House of Commons,
'So long as I am here you need not ask your Dad. You can
ask your Grand-dad.'

But Churchill has more than a knowledge of international
affairs. He is a great and acknowledged master in the art of
war. Defence and foreign policy are really two aspects of
the same policy. It is Churchill's pre-eminence in both
defence and foreign affairs that makes him unique. Above all,
the man whom so many ignorant Socialists deride as being
hopelessly out-of-date, has always been more abreast of
modern scientific development, actual and potential, than
any Conservative or Labour leader. Churchill's scientific
adviser, Lord Cherwell (known as 'The Prof'), was unpopular
in some quarters. Having apparently little in common with
Churchill, being an austere teetotaller, he exercised great
influence. Personally I found him a man of exceptional
integrity and ability and quite devoid of personal ambition.
This partnership was of far greater importance than was
generally realised. On other matters Churchill could himself
assess the opinions and check the facts presented to him. On
scientific affairs he largely accepted Lord Cherwell's advice.

All this is strictly relevant to the issue of high-level
conversations. Unlike Attlee and Bevin, Churchill never
showed the slightest tendency to underestimate the atomic
bomb. He stated publicly more than once that it was the
atomic bomb which in his view had deterred the Russians
from post-war aggression in Europe.

It seems likely that Stalin shared Churchill's view of the
atomic bomb. It caused astonishment and consternation
among high-up Soviet officials as had nothing else. Just when

they felt themselves secure, possibly for the first time in their lives, the angel of fear returned, familiar companion for ever at their elbow. We now know that they had received an enormous amount of information from Communist spies and sympathisers. It seems likely that they had not assessed this information correctly. It may be that the more serious officials feared that they would be liquidated if they presented the reports of their agents and spies in the West. This may account for the surprise evinced in Moscow in August 1945. Unfortunately in a lesser way the West reciprocated. The senior officials concerned, without exception, reported that the Soviet Union could not develop an atomic bomb until 1952 or 1953 at the earliest. Churchill, although receiving this advice, was a little sceptical. He believed—as it turned out, correctly—that Stalin would give atomic energy greater priority than any other defence project and that he would be tireless in his efforts to confound the West by producing an atomic bomb in the shortest possible time.

The proposal for a conference of the Big Three was first made by Churchill in Edinburgh during the 1950 General Election. It certainly contributed to diminish the size of the Labour victory and it helped to win the 1951 General Election. I had discussed it on many occasions with Churchill, having been, for some three years at least, an enthusiastic advocate of it as the only possible method of solving the deadlock over atomic bombs and other weapons of mass destruction. Churchill was always insistent on the necessity of ensuring that Stalin should know how dreadful another world war would be. To avoid a war with the Soviet Union, Churchill would have been willing to go to any lengths. 'I have even thought', he said one day, 'we might send some of our young pilots in bombers over the Soviet Union to drop one token non-explosive atomic bomb on each of their major cities and so convince them that they must come to a true peace settlement with us. Perhaps through a mistake one or two of them might die. But if I sent young men in thousands to die over Germany in the cause of war, should I not risk the lives of a few young men for the cause of peace?'

I do not believe that he would have thought of this as a

practical expedient except in a dire emergency. But the idea is an extreme example of his overriding passion to secure lasting peace and to be bold and resolute in the attainment of that object. He was convinced that weakness and indecision will lead to war. His famous phrase at Fulton that the Soviet Union wants 'the fruits of war without war itself' has stood the test of time. He wished to convince the leaders of the Soviet Union that, if they continued with such a policy, they might find themselves involved in a war which they did not want.

In my view it is a tragedy that the attempt to reach a final settlement with the Soviet Union was not made during the period when the Americans possessed a monopoly of atomic bombs. We were too much concerned with numbers of troops on the ground, too little with the devastating weapons of which the U.S.A. had a monopoly and the vast industrial capacity of the West. Time was not on our side. The best hope of a settlement lay in a top-level approach to Stalin before the Soviet Union developed atomic bombs. Many Labour members to whom I talked also supported the proposal. But Ernest Bevin was against it and even described Churchill's election speech as a stunt. Today the Labour Party are enthusiastic in support of the very idea they rejected time and again.

Churchill's insistence on the importance of atomic warfare dates from his decision at the beginning of the war to proceed with atomic research. He agreed to the bomb being dropped on Hiroshima, but was not consulted over the second bomb dropped on Nagasaki. This fateful decision—probably the most important of all those made by him—does not appear to trouble him. In 1947 I took Augustus John down to Chartwell to draw Churchill. We arrived at about eleven o'clock and the 'cher maître', as Churchill called him, worked away until lunch-time. During luncheon John said practically nothing, but afterwards when he had warmed up a bit, we witnessed a characteristic outburst. The subject of the atomic bomb on Hiroshima had been mentioned and John exploded.

It was, he said, the most monstrous crime in all history. We looked at Churchill, thinking he might be annoyed. But he was quite unperturbed and said, 'I have many things worse than that on my conscience.' This quiet and humble reply closed the subject. Churchill refused John's offer to give him the drawing which was afterwards sold for 250 guineas. He regards John as a very great master but criticised the drawing as putting too much below, i.e., under his chin, and too little on top. He atoned for the criticism with great charm. 'It is strange to think, *cher maître*, they will be looking at my ugly face a thousand years hence because you have drawn it.'

One thinks of Churchill as being modest, but he really is the Greek ideal, 'the man with a great soul', the man who assesses himself correctly. Many thousands and probably millions of people have said that but for Churchill Britain would have succumbed to Hitler in 1940. Not only does he deny this indignantly in private, but he has made it clear in the great book which he has written that Germany could not have succeeded if they had invaded in 1940. Yet he well knows the great affection with which he is regarded by Europeans as well as his own countrymen. In 1947 a delegation of trade unionists from Holland were being entertained in this country. Mark Hewitson, the National Organiser of the Municipal and General Workers Union, took them to the House of Commons and after lunch they went into the Strangers' Bar over which Ernest Bevin's friends Doris and Vera preside. It was a Thursday and therefore likely that Churchill would be in the smoke room. Mark Hewitson came to me and said that almost all of their trade unionists had been in the resistance movement. He wanted them to see Bevin but was not sure he could succeed. Would it be possible, he said, for me to get Churchill to see them?

I went immediately up to the smoke room where Churchill was seated in his usual chair reading the *Evening Standard*. I asked him if he could go down to the Strangers' Bar to see the delegation. The then Deputy Chief Whip, Patrick Buchan-Hepburn, was near him and he rose from his chair and summoned Buchan-Hepburn to come with him. I have never witnessed such a scene as ensued. When Churchill entered the Strangers' Bar, these hardy Dutchmen could hardly believe their eyes. Before he could open his mouth more than half of them broke into tears, so great was their feeling for him. But what really astonished me was the handsome face of Patrick Buchan-Hepburn, who looks the perfect picture of an English gentleman. I saw a tear trickle from his eye—much to his own dismay. This struck me as irresistibly humorous, and when Churchill returned to the smoke room for a whisky and soda, I told him about it. The next day Buchan-Hepburn was appointed Chief Whip. *Post hoc sed quaere propter hoc?*

Churchill derives great strength from his happy family life. Unlike many great men in history, he has been an outstanding example of filial, marital and paternal loyalty. His pride in all members of his family is intense. His wife is a most dignified and handsome lady to whom he is devoted. Unfortunately I never got on well with her. She thought me stupid, partly because I once declined to comment on the vexed subject of Palestine on the ground that I knew nothing about it. Thereafter I saw her rarely and on one occasion Churchill even championed, in her presence, my right to visit him. She has been of immense help to him but I always felt that, unlike her husband, she is an old-fashioned Tory and disapproves of the more buccaneering aspects of his life.

Churchill entertains great affection for his son Randolph, who has all his father's courage. His family circle embraces a large number of animals of different kinds, from bulls to butterflies. Perhaps the most extraordinary are the goldfish in what he calls his 'Bamboo grove'. These are very large and in the summer at about six or seven o'clock he would go to the pool and bark at the water's edge until the fish came towards him. He would then feed them, saying, 'And they say that fish can't hear!'

A possible alternative explanation is that the goldfish recognised the famous figure from previous experience of his generosity.

He loves to quote Robert Burns:
> 'To raise a happy fireside clime
> To weans and wife
> That's the true pathos and sublime
> Of human life.'

This is, oddly enough, the only poem by a first-class poet which I have heard him quote. The natural bent of his mind in this respect is towards the good second-class poets— Arthur Hugh Clough, Robert Louis Stevenson and others. Even music-hall songs and rhymes he recites with great gusto and enjoyment.

Baldwin and he were both dunces at Harrow, but unlike Baldwin he never afterwards became a classical scholar. Perhaps that has helped to keep his English pure and simple. An original must always be better than an imitation and few who have fallen under the spell of Greek thought and poetry can fail to imitate it consciously or unconsciously.

It is very difficult to assess the foundation of his strength and courage. He is not 'anchored on the steadfast rock of immortality'. I once asked him if he believed in personal survival and he said that he did not think so. It is obviously not a subject which exercises his mind. Yet somewhat paradoxically (as he admitted) he believes in one God who presides over the destinies of the Universe. There can be no doubt that this belief sustained him in 1940 when at times all must have seemed lost. Perhaps the man in the street is right in comparing Churchill to a bulldog. If so, his courage is a natural phenomenon and dependent on no faith or vision.

His ruthlessness has been shown by his publication of a telegram which he sent to the King at the time of his visit to Moscow. In this telegram he wrote concerning the London Polish Government, 'Our London lot as you know are decent but feeble.' He now knows perfectly well that these wounding words (which even appear to bring before the public the personal opinions of the late King) are quite untrue. Mikolayczyk went back to Poland largely as a result of Churchill's own persuasion and faced death and torture. I dined with Eden at Lady Cunard's apartment when the danger to Mikolayczyk was greatest. He said with characteristic integrity that if Mikolayczyk were to die, Churchill and he would be largely responsible. After Mikolayczyk's escape, I arranged an all-party meeting of M.P.s for him, at which Churchill took the chair. Although to my astonishment Churchill did not appear very interested to meet Mikolay-

czyk again in private, he paid a fine tribute to his courage and
patriotism. He must feel that both Britain and himself
owe an immense debt to Poland and that—perhaps uninten-
tionally—we have been parties to one of the greatest acts
of betrayal in all history. Indeed, after Yalta he sent Harold
Macmillan to see General Anders in Italy. More than half
of General Anders' troops, then fighting so well and so
bravely, came from that part of Poland which under the
Yalta agreement was to be incorporated in the U.S.S.R.
Churchill instructed Macmillan to tell Anders that he would
understand it if the Poles decided not to continue fighting.
The reply was that the Poles who had fought with us in
1940 when we stood alone would continue to fight for us
even after we had agreed to half their country being incorporated in the Soviet Union. Macmillan told me that the
extraordinary loyalty of the Poles at this time was beyond
belief. Yet Churchill, whom Macmillan idolises, decided to
publish a telegram in which he described the Polish leaders
as 'decent but feeble'. Such is his ruthlessness in the attainment of his object—in this case to write a great book, on
other occasions, fortunately for ourselves, to save Britain from
disaster. Genius is almost invariably born out of ruthlessness
such as Churchill can display when determined to reach his
objective.

Unlike the great Duke, Churchill did not exhaust his
glory, but wore it with an almost rakish air, with a surprising
humility, and with gratitude towards his countrymen. He
had the good fortune to attain supreme power when time
had mellowed his impetuosity and experience had enriched
his genius. He has taken his place among the heroes whose
legend is written not in tablets nor in bronze but in the
hearts of men.

CHAPTER IX

The Labour Leaders

I ENTERED Parliament at the same time as most of the present
Labour leaders—Gaitskell, Wilson, Robens, Callaghan
and others. They are not easy to describe as individuals.
Perhaps the new leaders in the new age are so much tied up
with Party tactics, Party loyalty and bureaucracy that they
have no distinctive personalities to describe. To one another,
of course, they must and do appear very different. Callaghan
was at one time sufficiently left-wing to have supported the
cause of the affiliation of the Communist Party to the Labour
Party. He nearly joined the 'Keep Left' Group and expressly
left them on grounds of tactics and Party loyalty. Hence his
nickname of 'Slim Jim'. Robens is a friendly, warm-hearted
member of the Co-operative Party, whose back-slapping
technique—I write figuratively—conceals a sincere desire
to help his fellow-man. Gaitskell and Wilson are both
bureaucrats of differing degrees of ability. Some of these men
are sometimes charged with conceit when, in fact, they give
that appearance through being either too shy or too unsure
of themselves. In any event, no one would suggest that they
possess the great character or personality of the men who
are an easy target for many pens—Churchill, Bevin, Bevan.

Bevan, however, underestimated Gaitskell in describing
him as a 'desiccated calculating machine'. The word
'desiccated' was inaccurate as well as redundant. That this
was so I saw on the night when Hugh Dalton invited about
ten of the promising young men of the Party to a private
dinner at St Ermine's immediately after the 1945 General
Election—and before all Ministerial appointments had been
made. The subject of the kind of men who should obtain the
junior Ministerial appointments came up for discussion.

Two or three of us said—I remember Callaghan was one—
that it seemed only fair that those who had borne the heat
and burden of the day in Opposition should be given the
chance of office and should at least have the consolation of
knowing that at one time they had earned their Second
Eleven Colours. At this Gaitskell courageously said, 'Our
responsibilities are too great to allow Government Departments to be run by men who do not know how to run them.
Before very long those who know how to control civil
servants will be required in any event. Why should they
not be blooded immediately and so prove of great help to the
senior Ministers who can so easily be baffled by their senior
civil servants?' Gaitskell was certainly not 'desiccated' on
that occasion and before long he was in a key position as
Parliamentary Secretary to the Ministry of Fuel and Power,
where after the coal crisis there was much prestige to be
gained. Soon he became Minister of Fuel and Power and
delivered cogent speeches showing a mastery of paper-work
and political argument such as was very rare in any Minister.

Gaitskell had been Private Secretary to Hugh Dalton and
then had been promoted by Dalton to an important executive position at the Board of Trade. He was an excellent civil
servant, particularly assiduous at doing the will of his
'master'—as he, as a private secretary, called his friend
Hugh Dalton. He learned a great deal from Dalton, whose
intelligence and gift of speech has for some extraordinary
reason never been correctly assessed by the Press or the
general public. But unlike Dalton he lived a quiet, austere
life, was never seen in the smoking room and by dint of
hard work and reliability found his way into the favour of
Attlee and Cripps. Cripps groomed him for succession to the
Chancellorship and so to the chance of being the future
Labour leader. Once he was Chancellor he continued the
policies of his predecessor. He struck a decisive blow in
relation to his chances of becoming the Party leader by
insisting on a minor economy in the Health Service after
Bevan had said that he would resign from the Government
if it was introduced. The latent hostility between Attlee and
Bevan—nothing like so great as that between Morrison and

Bevin, but nevertheless a factor of great importance at this time—was sparked off. Bevan resigned, as he was bound to do if he kept his promise, but he gave as his main reason the inflated size of the defence programme which, he rightly said, was not only wasteful and unnecessary, but actually beyond the power of industry to fulfil. By resigning Bevan swung 'the machine' against him and became very unpopular among Labour members. The fact that he was right and Gaitskell wrong over the defence programme, and that it was the Chancellor's duty to curb Government expenditure, did not avail Bevan. Gaitskell had earned Attlee's loyalty. Later Attlee was to repay the debt by hanging on to the Labour leadership long enough to kill the chances of the ageing Morrison and leave the crown to fall into Gaitskell's lap. All this, of course, could not have occurred if Gaitskell, in addition to being an orthodox right-wing Socialist acceptable to the leaders of the T.U.C., had not also been a consistently effective debater, always bringing out new points damaging to the Tories.

Gaitskell comes of a family with a fine record of service to the British Empire. The natural bent of his mind, as shown in his first speech over Suez, is to present a pro-British rather than a Socialist foreign policy. But he will be unable to maintain the leadership of the Party in substance as well as in name unless he either moves substantially to the left or he produced something of the genius which Bevan undoubtedly possesses. He is a more intelligent man than Attlee and a better debater, but otherwise he belongs to much the same mould. The tasks which he faces are formidable. If Socialism does not destroy bureaucracy, bureaucracy will destroy Socialism. Yet Socialists are *ex hypothesi* men who believe in the efficacy of State planning, that is of more and more intervention by civil servants—and Gaitskell is himself by training and nature a bureaucrat. Moreover, in the task of overriding left-wing prejudices he has not the advantage either of being a Bevin or of having anyone with the ability of Bevin to back him. He has not a pleasing personality and this may well be a greater handicap to him than to Attlee in the television era. Nevertheless, there are

very powerful factors which should keep him firmly in the
saddle—the Labour tradition of Party loyalty, the centri-
fugal tendency which develops among Labour M.P.s when
they fear a Tory landslide, the backing of some able trade
unionists, such as Tom Williamson, and his own cool head
and persuasive tongue.

But the man who really makes the running in the Labour
Party is Aneurin Bevan. Ever since 1944 he has been the
hero of the constituency parties. He has not only the Health
Service to his credit, but the reputation for being the real
heir to the traditions of Keir Hardie and the pioneers of
Socialism. Before 1945 the Fabians used to decry Bevan as
'oppositional'. Many people prophesied that administration
would be his downfall. But at least in the eyes of the Socialists
the reverse proved to be the case. His appeal to the heart of
the Labour Party was supplemented by what appeared to be
great tactical ability as a Minister, notably in dealing with
the members of the medical profession who were hostile
to his proposed Health Service. It was no mean achievement
to secure the support of *The Times* in his favour against the
representatives of the medical profession. In fact, of course,
the Bevan Health Scheme has put an enormous amount of
money into the pockets of general practitioners and dentists,
which they would never have seen otherwise. From the
financial point of view the Royal College of Physicians should
erect a statue in his honour to show their gratitude. But to
Labour supporters he seemed to have scored a great victory
over the diehards in the medical profession.

After Churchill and Bevin he must be regarded as the
most sincere man among the great political figures of the
century. Neither Churchill nor Bevin was ever prepared to
compromise over major issues of national policy, when they
were convinced they were in the right. The same holds good
of Bevan, with the possible exception of the 1947-1950
period, when he was often in fundamental opposition to his
colleagues. He has never shown care for his own skin, when
his convictions were profound enough. Over and over again
he has flouted the advice of his most intimate friends and
done things which deeply shocked even moderate opinion

in the Labour Party—as over Regulation 1AA—the anti-strike regulation during the war—and over the manner of his resignation from the Government in 1951. It is inconceivable that he was inspired in these actions by motives of personal self-advancement which are utterly alien to his character. On the face of it he appeared to be committing political suicide—and he knew it and counted it nothing compared with the duty of telling the truth as he saw it. The same was true of Churchill over the abdication crisis. Mean petty men say of Bevan as they said of Churchill that on such occasions he 'misjudged the temper of the House of Commons'. The fact is that they were not concerned with 'the temper of the House of Commons'. They were concerned to do what they thought right, although the majority of their countrymen might have been in passionate disagreement with them.

Although Bevan's speeches are sometimes extreme, he is not an extremist. The public is regaled from time to time by what they regard as typical Bevanisms—that 'the Tories are lower than vermin' and similar remarks. Occasionally these outbursts do occur, no doubt because some immediate irritation arouses old and bitter memories. His father died, in his arms, of pneumoconiosis which was not then accepted as an industrial disease incidental to mining. But when he makes moderate remarks they are not reported, even on occasions when one might expect it. I was the speaker to precede him at the opening meeting for the Birmingham Labour Party at the 1950 General Election. I deliberately dealt in his presence with the subject of nationalisation and said that the Labour Party had no intention of nationalising all industry as it recognised the danger of totalitarianism arising from such a programme. I went further and said that the only justification for nationalising private industry was lack of enterprise on the part of that industry or the denial to the workers in that industry of their fair share of the profits. Bevan, after listening to that part of my speech, went out of his way before a horde of reporters (foreign and domestic) to approve my speech specifically and to reproduce the same theme in his own words. I was naturally delighted, as he explicitly refuted the ideological approach to the matter and accepted the need for empirical justification of nationalisation. Not one word of that part of his speech appeared in any newspaper. Bevan had spoken like Macmillan and was not considered newsworthy.

His relations with the Press have been unfortunate, although he has friends among journalists and shared a flat at one time with Frank Owen. On one occasion I showed him something which had been written about him which was manifestly untrue and libellous. I pointed out to him that he could force a withdrawal of it and a public apology. He said that it would be the height of folly for him to chase the lies that were being told about him and Jennie Lee, his wife. He does not even bother to contradict false reports about his movements and activities. Perhaps it is right that a man who is himself a master of vituperative invective should have a very thick skin.

He is an extraordinarily warm-hearted man. He shares with Eden the apparently effeminate habit of addressing other men as 'my dear', but in his case there is more feeling behind the use of the words and one does not draw the impression, as with Eden, that it is a mere affectation. In August 1944 I visited him at his house and he suggested that my wife (whom he had not met) should come up from Camberley where she was living and spend the night, although it meant her sharing a room with Jennie and his sharing a room with me. When my wife arrived with me by taxi, he emerged from his house and embraced her before I had had the chance to introduce them. It was done with such a natural grace and such obvious goodwill that my wife and I laughed our heads off. I cannot imagine anyone else who would have done the same thing without causing embarrassment or annoyance.

When I first met Bevan, he was in the greatest danger of being expelled from the Labour Party for constantly voting against the Party Whip and above all for attacking the Party leaders. He had just called Morrison 'a third-rate Tammany boss'. But neither the entreaties of his friends nor the threats of his enemies could deter him from his course. His speeches are almost entirely extempore and he can easily be carried

away by his delight in words. Churchill has learned to depart
only rarely and with discretion from his prepared text.
Bevan is, therefore, the better debater in the strict sense of
the word. Indeed, during the period from 1945 to 1951
Churchill never clashed directly with Bevan, whose Parliamentary performances delighted the Labour benches and
even drove the Tories into staying away from the end of the
debates when he was winding up.

The strange thing is that although Bevan has a great
reputation among Socialists abroad and has followers at
home described as Bevanites, it is not possible to define
Bevanism. The Webbs used to divide Socialists into the A's
and the B's—those who were anarchist and those who were
bureaucratic in tendency. Bevan is undoubtedly an Anar-
chist-Socialist and is the enemy of the Bureaucrat-Socialists.
The Communists are, of course, the furthest removed of all
from the Anarchist-Socialists, yet Bevan has the reputation
of being closer to the Communists than any other important
Labour leader. Bevan was fêted in India, and praising
Nehru, advocated the great advantage in international
affairs of having 'a third force' to keep the peace between the
Soviet and the American camps. The next day Nehru
repudiated the whole idea which, he said, was not a correct
representation of his policy. The appeal of India was not to
the arbitrament of force but to the conscience of the world.
India could not and would not place herself at the head of any
group of nations seeking to become a balancing power
between the Soviet area of the world and the Western
countries. It was all very puzzling, as Bevan had been a
member of the Labour Government which explicitly
renounced the doctrine of the 'third force'.

Bevan does not really support any consistent policies or
principle. He represents the spirit of revolt against all in
modern Socialism which appears to dehumanise it, particularly against measures taken at the instance of the
Treasury, which cut across Socialist idealism. He mistrusts
the planners by instinct and is now doubly hateful to them
because office gave him the opportunity to realise how great
is the gap between the world as Whitehall depicts it in

official files and statistics and the actual world we live in. Oddly enough, there are many subjects on which Aneurin Bevan and Sir Leonard Lord would see eye to eye. It is a great pity that Bevan has not been willing to learn more from practical industrialists who are hostile to bureaucracy. Those whom the Labour Party used, such as Lord Heyworth of Lever Brothers, who recommended the nationalisation of the electrical industry, are men with a natural belief in huge combines which themselves resemble in many respects the nationalised industries. They are not genuine upholders of free enterprise. They themselves have an excessive faith in planning. The Tories did not often mention that the Labour Government's ground-nuts scheme was largely based on the report of a nominee of Lever Brothers.

Bevan has a very powerful personality. His infectious laughter usually exceeds that of anyone at the same table, even when the jokes are his own. The only person to whom he listens respectfully without contradiction is his very attractive wife, Jennie Lee. She is really left-wing, with absolute faith in the cause of Socialism and very little faith in Labour organisations. Her irony and sarcasm are powerful weapons from a good-looking woman whose coolness can be barbed. I once heard her in a Party meeting get a number of laughs at the expense of Ernest Bevin, who listened good-humouredly and with respect. Probably no other Labour Member could have done the same. Like her husband, she is utterly without 'side' and is a very kind person. Of all the political couples I have met, 'Nye' and 'Jennie' are outstanding as the sort of people one would want to know and to have as friends, if politics were not their main preoccupation. They are generous, loyal and understanding in their personal relationships. After I left the Labour Party, I had occasion to lead a delegation to the then Minister of Health, Aneurin Bevan. I had not seen him since my defection from the Party and wondered how I should be treated. He went out of his way to be even more friendly than usual and did not show by a glance, let alone by a phrase, that he was aware that I was no longer a member of the same Party as himself. To all outward appearances I was a colleague whose

representations he would accept, if possible, and reject, if
need be, with the greatest regret. The attitude of some other
Labour Ministers, particularly junior Ministers, was very
different.

A few of his friends prophesy that he will be Prime
Minister one day. They overlook the fact that once a man
has antagonised 'the machine', that is the Party organisation
and those who work in it and control it, he can never command the support of that Party unless he is in effect 'drafted'
into 10 Downing Street by popular opinion and by the
votes of opposing parties supporting a minority in his own
Party. This is what happened to Churchill only after he had
proved right again and again, and Chamberlain had been
discredited in the eyes of many of his own former supporters.
The crucial fact in Churchill's favour was that the Labour
and Liberal Parties would serve in a Coalition under him
but not under Chamberlain. It seems unlikely that a parallel
situation should occur in favour of 'Nye' Bevan with the
Tories demanding that he should supersede Gaitskell—even
if this country were to face again a danger recognised to be as
great as that of 1940.

Without attaining supreme office, Bevan may yet prove
to have had a much greater effect than most men who
become Prime Minister. Churchill described him as 'a
squalid nuisance' during the war period. Nevertheless,
whatever the merits of his many controversial contributions
to debate, he helped to keep the House of Commons alive
when without him and a few others such as 'Dick' Stokes it
might have become a mere rubber-stamp for the Government. He performed the same service for the Labour
Party just when it seemed to be becoming rigid and conservative. Any man who is strong enough to stand up against
the caucus of either Party without appealing to totalitarian
sentiment has deserved well of his country and his Party—
even though he has often been sadly misguided. If Bevan had
been given the chance to direct affairs as Prime Minister, he
might well have surprised everybody. Another eloquent
Welshman, once denounced as 'a little Englander' and an
opponent of the Boer War, proved to be a doughty fighter at

international conferences in favour of the British Commonwealth and Empire. I personally am convinced that in
supreme office Bevan would have moved very rapidly away
from the so-called Bevanites and would have pursued a
realistic policy. Moreover, unlike Gaitskell, he would have
been in a particularly strong position to withstand attacks
from the left wing. As it is, circumstances force him to
remain to some extent the victim of his own romantic nature.

The struggle between Gaitskell and his supporters on the
one hand and Bevan and his sympathisers on the other is
not simply a matter of conflicting ambitions and personalities. Nor is it fundamentally a tug of war between the trade
unions with their practical approach and the constituency
parties with their idealistic approach to Socialism. Bevan
has a large following in many sections of the trade union
movement. But it is remarkably difficult to say exactly what
the struggle is about, because the opposing forces seem to be
continually changing their ground. When the Tories are
in power, the Labour Party and therefore Gaitskell seem
often to adopt the very line which Bevan advocated unsuccessfully when Labour itself was in power. Perhaps the issue
is more one of the way policies are administered than of the
policies themselves. An industry can be nationalised in such
a way as to make very little, if any, difference to the workers
in that industry—as happened with the railways. Bevan
wants a revolutionary method of putting into effect policies
which profess to be revolutionary. He would not have put
Lord Hyndley in charge of the Coal Board or S. J. L. Hardie
in charge of the Steel Board. By temperament he is opposed
to the managerial revolution which seems to characterise
the private as well as the public sector of industry. He has
sympathy with syndication and favours devolution as against
the concentration of power in the hands of Ministers and their
civil servants. He would put the need for social justice before
consistency in planning and even before efficiency. If a fully
Socialist state were to emerge, there would be much more
room for manoeuvre by individuals under Bevan than under
Gaitskell. Yet, in the event of failure, it would be more difficult to unscramble the eggs after Bevan had been the cook

than after Gaitskell. For he says that in the last resort 'politics is war', however strong friendships may be between those on different sides.

Even so, Bevan remains an unpredictable character. His fellow Welshman, W. G. Cove, says that as a young man in the pits he would read books when he ought to be working and then suddenly hack away at the coalface like a man possessed until he had made up the arrears. He possesses similar powers of recovery in the political field. 'I know', he once said to me, 'that I was put in the Cabinet, not because they wanted me there, but because they thought me too dangerous outside.' The Press often concentrates more on his obvious defects than on his positive virtues. Yet as he himself said, 'Men are more often lured to their doom by their virtues than by their vices'. It will be a sad day for the Labour Party if Bevan's outspokenness should ever really send him into the wilderness. Then indeed much of the life would go out of its affairs; there is no one with the fire or the courage or the imagination to replace him, and the field would be left to the dull bureaucrats and the intelligentsia who, in their hearts, agree with Crossman: 'It is not a question of dictatorship. Dictatorship is inevitable in the modern state.'

Of course, Bevan is now getting old. The only youthful figure acquiring any of the Bevan magic in the eyes of Socialists is Michael Foot, a lovable fanatic with a sense of humour. His record against Communism as well as Fascism is excellent althouth he has many suspect political friends. At least he is a great champion of freedom, and as long as he is a darling of the left, there is some eventual hope of it being rescued from the bureaucrats.

CHAPTER X

The Rôle of an Independent

I DO not wish to imply that alcoholics (including myself in particular) perform no useful services because of the disease to which slowly but inexorably they become victims. In active service I found the drunks to be among the best fighting soldiers. As for myself, I have written so much of what I did wrong that perhaps I may be forgiven if I write a little of the things which I believe I did right.

My great mistake was to believe that I could keep my public and my private life in strictly separate compartments. I thought that my overwhelmingly important duty was to show integrity and moral courage in my public life. I believed that I was showing a higher concentration of these qualities than is common among politicians who recognise their first duty as being to their party and who are for the most part content to leave matters to 'those who know best'.

If in my private life I was an excessivist, living and loving too hard and too fast, that, I hoped, was my own affair. But unfortunately no such spiritual dichotomy is possible. What a man does becomes part of him. The causes in which I believed suffered to some extent, however small, because one who espoused them publicly was becoming in private a hedonist and a drunkard. But even so, I was able from time to time to achieve a number of things because I was at heart an independent and because I was willing to use my powers of expression without fear or favour.

My main interest in Parliament related to freedom and to science. I realised very early in my political life that Communism for all its positive qualities would mean in the long run the destruction of the spirit of man. I did not then realise sufficiently that even within the western democracies

there is an insidious erosion of freedom, although from time
to time I fought against encroachments on personal freedom.
But so far as the external danger of the spread of Communism
across Europe was concerned, I was among the first on the
Labour benches to be outspoken and uncompromising. At
that time many Labour members would have agreed with
what one of the present five leading members of the Labour
Party said to me. 'Raymond, you are a good fellow. Why
do you not realise that in the last resort the Communists are
our allies and the Tories are our enemies?'

Yet while I was a passionate opponent of Communism, I
was not unaware of its achievements. As early as November
30th, 1945, I warned the House of Commons of the extent
of the Soviet effort in atomic energy—having been given
some information which afterwards proved correct. I knew
that the priority given to this subject in the Soviet Union
was even higher than that given to it in the U.S.A. or
Britain. I said, 'In the Soviet Union there is an entirely
different system. Its interest . . . in nuclear research today is
ahead of that in the United States or Great Britain.' Unfortunately the matter did not rest there. 'In 1938-9 our total
research expenditure was just over £1,000,000, but the
total research expenditure in the U.S.A. was just on
£10,000,000. The university expenditure . . . amounts to
less than one tenth of the equivalent expenditure in the
U.S.A. I believe the same would apply to the Soviet Union.'
In this debate and during the following years I advocated
not only increased expenditure on research but a National
Research Council to co-ordinate and promote research and
development in the Universities, in Government Departments, and in industry. In retrospect it seems incredible that
the Labour Government which was elected to introduce a
planned economy took so little interest in scientific research
and development except in relation to the nationalised
industries. One reason why I came to believe that the return
of Churchill as Prime Minister would benefit the country
was his interest in scientific development and his intimate
friendship with Lord Cherwell. Cherwell was committed to
the creation of a technical university, but even he could not

get his way when Churchill came back to power. Not till recently has the need for increasing the number of our scientists and technicians been recognised.

One amusing incident in the November 1945 debate on science which I initiated in the House of Commons related to the composition of the House itself. In an aside I said: 'It is perhaps a little unfortunate that we have something like eighty lawyers in the House and I do not think a single scientist.' At that a barrister named Solley, afterwards expelled from the Labour Party for his near-Communist activities, leaped to his feet and claimed to be a scientist. This intervention caused some amusement, but to my astonishment Mr Solley was not the only M.P. to challenge my statement. Mr Arthur Palmer, afterwards a close and esteemed colleague of mine, said that he was an engineer and might claim to be in some sense a scientist. Another M.P. said that there were ten who were members of the Association of Scientific Workers. This, of course, meant little or nothing. (Hugh Gaitskell was one.) I was able to conclude the matter by saying as loudly as I could: 'I said that there is not as far as I know one M.P. who is still primarily a scientist; by that I mean an honourable gentleman who makes his living out of scientific processes and scientific inventions'. I was, of course, right. The only Fellow of the Royal Society was Sir John Anderson, who for all his scientific knowledge never claimed to be a scientist. Good as is the work of the Parliamentary and Scientific Committee, it still seems to me that there should be a member of scientists in the House and that there are far too many lawyers who are more likely than other Members to regard Parliament as a help in their careers rather than as a vocation.

It would be wrong for the general reader if I were to go into details about the work which I undertook for the Parliamentary and Scientific Committee, of which I was Joint Honorary Secretary for five years and Deputy Chairman for a year. As Chairman of its Coal Utilisation Committee I had serving under me two former Ministers, one of them Gwilym Lloyd George who was later to be Home Secretary when I was a prisoner and was to reject in that

capacity all petitions which I made to enable my case to be
the subject of an independent review. We had some achievements to our credit, notably obtaining Prime Minister's list
priority for machinery for the better utilisation of fuel. But
the one legislative achievement for which, I believe, some of
us were responsible was the National Research Development
Corporation. The sequel to our success was most instructive.

It has often and widely been alleged that there are many
inventions which are suppressed because industry is unable
or unwilling to finance them for reasons of its own. Alec
Guiness appeared in a most amusing film, 'The Man in the
White Suit', written around this theme, in which the
inventor of a suit which will not wear out or get dirty
finds himself hated by employers and employees alike
because he will not agree to the suppression of his invention. For many years we campaigned in public and in private
that there should be some public corporation able to finance
the development of inventions which private enterprise was
unable or unwilling to undertake, provided that the development of the invention appeared to be in the public interest.
I even tackled the Prime Minister in the smoke room
about it, only to receive the usual reply that the matter
was under consideration. But both Arthur Greenwood and
Hugh Dalton were strong supporters and Herbert Morrison
had agreed to do his best to get our idea put into practice.
Eventually the great day came and the National Research
Development Corporation (founded primarily to exploit
discoveries made by scientists engaged in Government
Departments) was given the added duty of helping inventors
in the circumstances which I have described. Here was a
great chance for Harold Wilson as President of the Board
of Trade to appoint really progressive men, whatever their
political views, who would be willing to take risks for the
advancement of British science.

In the year after their appointment, the Board of Direc-
tors received many hundreds of applications. In only one
case did they take any practical action and in only three
cases did they fail to reject the applications either directly or
by shelving them. In some ways this was my most dis-

heartening experience in my public life. I knew, and in one specific case proved, that there were important British scientific discoveries being retarded or even stifled for lack of money. The Board ruled that if a discovery were of such a nature that the City of London would normally be expected to finance it, the Development Corporation would not compete with the City. This ruling entirely defeated the purpose of this part of the Act. Everyone was very friendly to me about it, knowing the part I had played in getting the Research Corporation established. But I could get no action. Government Corporations resemble Government Departments in their strict and essentially negative approach to their duties. Wherever positive action is demanded the natural tendency is to play safe and search for reasons why that action should not be taken. Oliver Lyttleton (now Lord Chandos) quipped: 'The road to Carey Street is paved with good inventions'. But there are worse recommendations for a man than that he got to Carey Street. Handel went bankrupt for writing *The Messiah*, the most successful piece of music ever composed. William Pitt died £40,000 in debt. Frieze-Green, inventor of cinematography, was almost always hopelessly insolvent, and so were scores of other men who have made immense contributions to science, to art and to letters. They have more than squared their accounts with posterity. Real progress almost always demands the taking of risks, sometimes even the taking of uncalculated risks. Until such a spirit infuses our Government Corporations they are certain to be failures by comparison with private enterprise, even though that private enterprise is so often sadly unenterprising.

Throughout my years in the House of Commons I was tormented by the knowledge that time was not on our side. Almost all the members of the House seemed to accept that so long as Communism was defeated in Britain and in America and efforts were made to help the democratic elements in Western Europe, we were bound to prevail in the long run. The exclusive American possession of the atomic bomb lulled many people into a false sense of security. In the speech I made immediately after my resignation from the

Labour Party in the late summer of 1950 I said: 'The great events of the world take place when men are asleep. . . . The whole difference between this period and any other comparable period in our history is that today time marches against us with relentless rapidity.' During that year the Soviet Union developed atomic bombs years before anyone expected and the whole of China went Communist. In the session of the House of Commons when these events occurred, neither was specifically debated. The Members were concerned with domestic matters and above all with the prospects of a General Election. The Party system is now so rigid and so dominant that the main issues are left to the Party leaders who decide how the whips shall be issued.

When we went to war over Korea I saw how little influence individual Members of Parliament, let alone their constituents, are able to exert on those in authority even where the great issues are at stake.

By 1950 all who were not wilfully blind had seen the pattern of Soviet expansionism. I have always been of the opinion that the death of Petkov marked the point of no return—the more so because Bulgaria is a Slav country and traditionally pro-Russian. But the evidence that the Soviet Union was imposing its will ruthlessly wherever its soldiers were in occupation accumulated until it became almost unbelievable. Perhaps Poland and Czechoslovakia were the outstanding examples. Few would then have thought that Hungary would have been the first European country to rise against its alien rulers and their quislings and to display heroism which will shine in history for all its failure. The Berlin blockade and a host of minor incidents—kidnappings, murders, torturings and just plain insults—had shown that the Soviet Union pursued aggressive policies falling just short of war. It was also clear that if Stalin was allowed to win a victory over the West, his appetite would be stimulated and a major war would become inevitable. Stalin had the immense advantage of having satellite states which could be used for the purpose of exploiting the situation to the full without incurring direct risks to the Soviet Union itself.

The exact relationship between China and the Soviet

Union remains wrapped in mystery. It is not therefore certain whether North Korea should be regarded as a satellite of the Soviet Union or of its ally China. For all practical purposes it made no difference at the time. On June 26th, 1950, the Prime Minister announced in the House of Commons that the invasion of South Korea by North Korea had taken place. The 38th Parallel had been crossed in a number of places. In the absence of the Soviet representatives the Security Council had passed a resolution calling for the immediate cessation of hostilities and denouncing the invasion as a breach of the peace. I had spoken to a few Members before the announcement and could not assess what the mood of the House would be. The general attitude seemed to be that such supreme issues as those of peace and war must be left to those who know best, although some Labour members were obviously against war in any circumstances. (There is a hard core of fifty pacifists or near-pacifists in the Parliamentary Labour Party.) When Mr Attlee sat down Mr Churchill said: 'We shall be grateful if the Prime Minister will keep us informed from day to day on this matter?' This sounded non-committal and un-Churchillian, but as the Leader of the Opposition he was inhibited.

I was absolutely certain that the Korean aggression should be resisted and I was resolved to take any action open to me, however extreme, to help in seeing that the British Government would play a leading part in the resistance of the aggression. But I was anxious not to prejudice the cause by an ill-tried or rash intervention. On this day I said nothing. A Conservative Member, to the horror of all sides of the House, advocated the dropping of an atomic bomb on the capital of North Korea. The fact that the House was utterly opposed to any such action did not, however, mean that it would oppose resistance by the use of conventional force. So far as I could tell, the House on June 26th had not made up its mind what action should be taken. I spoke to dozens of my colleagues, Labour and Conservative, and found most of them undecided. I hoped that did not necessarily mean that they could not be persuaded. Seymour Cocks, Chairman of the Party's Foreign Affairs Committee

THE RÔLE OF AN INDEPENDENT 127

and generally regarded as left-wing, promised he would
support me the next day if I advocated armed resistance to
the invasion. His pre-war record in relation to Nazism had
been excellent.

The next day Members generally did not appear to be
decided. So at half past three, when the Prime Minister and
Mr Churchill both made somewhat inconclusive statements,
I rose and asked whether the Prime Minister was aware that
'there are many people in this country who believe that His
Majesty's Government should support the United States
under Article 47 of the Charter if they are prepared to take
action in collective self-defence with Southern Korea against
this monstrous invasion?' I said 'United States' and not
'United Nations' because I wished to be absolutely definite
about the resistance to the aggression. The Soviet Union
could send a representative to the United Nations and veto
any proposal. Why it did not do so will remain a mystery for
a long time. If one knew the answer to this mystery, it
would throw great light on Sino-Soviet relations. On the
face of it, it would almost appear that the Soviet Union
either did not know or did not wholly approve of the Korean
adventure, or that Stalin, having approved it, decided that
the Soviet Union itself must in public remain as remote as
possible from events. When I said 'United States' many
Members shouted 'United Nations'. Mr Churchill intervened immediately after me to prevent an answer by the
Prime Minister. He had obviously just been informed that
the great decision had already been taken by Truman on the
authority vested in him as President of the United States.
But other members did not know this, not even his colleagues.

After questions Harold Macmillan came up to me in the
smoke room and said: 'I know a certain amount of what has
been going on. If by this time tomorrow war has not been
declared I will support and sign a motion on the lines suggested in your question. Get the best Labour Members you
can to sign with you.' I told him about Seymour Cocks and
he was pleased and spoke of the days before the war when he
himself became an independent because he disapproved of
the foreign policies of the Chamberlain Government. Even

then he was a leading member of the Conservative Party and if he had done as he promised—and he certainly would never be a man to break his word—he might have gone for a time into the wilderness again. His attitude was strongly in contrast to that of a Conservative M.P. who said to me: 'I always admire your courage. But you were wrong today. However strongly you feel, on so grave an issue you should speak only in private and not embarrass your leaders.'

The incidents I have described were in fact irrelevant or abortive. Truman had already taken the vital decision, unknown to us. The Soviet Union did not use its veto. All else naturally followed. The United States bore the main brunt of the fighting and other countries sent forces which, although insignificant, were little more than token contributions to the defence of South Korea. The point which I submit arises is this: 'Even in the democracies how much influence can be exerted on Governments by ordinary people when the supreme issues of peace or war arise?' I am convinced that if President Truman had not take his historic decision, South Korea would have been overrun before the Parliaments of the West had decided that the aggression must be resisted. I am not even sure that the Parliaments would not have been content with pious resolutions and no action.

This does not mean that individual Members of Parliament, who can of course be persuaded by a constituent to take any action open to them, are entirely powerless. It is magnificent that in Britain, unlike the U.S.A., every Minister is accountable on the floor of the House for every action or inaction of his Department and must answer specific questions. Unfortunately Ministers all too often get away with inadequate and even incorrect answers. But the process of requiring civil servants to give precise answers which are printed in *Hansard* and may give rise to great publicity is very wholesome. The specific question which the Member asks is printed on the order paper for the day. Subject to the discretion of the Speaker other Members may ask other questions extempore on the same point. A Minister who cannot answer such questions and constantly says 'I must ask for

notice to be given of that question' is tacitly confessing that
he has not mastered the subject. There is probably no better
test of a Minister's competence than his ability to answer
supplementary questions.

One such question which I asked sparked off the row about
rubber to China in 1951 and led to a change in Government
policy. It is astonishing that this story is so little known or has
been forgotten.

The Korean War started in June 1950. Towards the end of
the year the United Nations forces pressed the North Koreans
back beyond the 38th Parallel and finally beyond 'the waist'
of Korea. Churchill believed they should have been stopped
at the waist and later said so. ('No good lover stops at the
waist', murmured Seymour Cocks, sitting at my side.)
The Chinese intervened in great strength and pushed the
United Nations back well below the 38th Parallel. The war
had become a war between China as well as North Korea
and the United Nations. America declared in December an
absolute embargo on exports to its enemy China. Britain did
not follow suit.

On May 2nd, 1951, Emanuel Shinwell as Minister of
Defence made a statement about the 'glorious Gloucesters'.
I had only just discovered a little of what had been happening, but I was so horrified that I was prepared to take this
opportunity of asking a question which might stop the shameful behaviour of the British Government. In a crowded
House I said: 'May I regretfully ask the Minister of Defence
whether he is aware that between January and March we
supplied the Chinese with thousands of tons of steel, with
locomotives, ships and aircraft, and whether it is not high
time we ceased to supply the people against whom our boys
are fighting in Korea with war materials?' Shinwell denied
this and said I was completely misinformed. After several
more questions on other subjects I was called again and read
out slowly and indignantly the Government's own figures
published in *Hansard* a few days before showing that between
January and March 1951 3,430 tons of iron and steel and
locomotives, ships and aircraft to the value of £71,000 had
been exported to China. (In fact, of course, 'Locomotives,

E

ships and aircraft' is a Board of Trade category and £71,000 worth, although appreciable, would not represent a great contribution to the Chinese war effort.) The Labour front bench was flabbergasted, although still hoping that Shinwell might have an answer. But he was pressed by other questions and Churchill was obviously right when he said to Shinwell: 'You do not know anything about it all'. I have never seen a worse performance at question time than this by Shinwell. The proceedings ended in uproar and the Speaker had to call the House to order.

Far worse was to come. The real profits made by this country out of selling strategic goods to the enemy it was fighting were enormous and were made out of rubber. Sir Hartley Shawcross had just been made President of the Board of Trade and he was the Minister charged with the duty of preparing the Government's brief and defending it. He did so throughout with extraordinary arrogance, which over and over again was rebuked by Churchill, and with consistent malice towards us. 'Promotion has gone to the head of the right honourable gentleman', said Churchill, when Shawcross tried to counter my facts by referring to my resignation from the Labour Party so that I was no longer a 'responsible' Member of the House. The series of questions led to a full debate initiated by Churchill, who personally intervened with the Deputy Speaker to have me called. This debate was held on May 10th—eight days after my supplementary—and the Government announced a change of policy and an embargo on exports to China.

But the conduct of Shawcross on this occasion, as on the occasion of the 'Dictatorship Bill', seemed to me to be so indifferent to the moral issues involved that I felt it must be wrong not to summarise the facts, which were as follows:

From January to June 1950 we exported 4,000 tons of rubber to China. From July to December 1950 we exported 73,000 tons of rubber to China. From January to March 1951 we exported 46,500 tons of rubber to China. Even in April 1951, when Shawcross claimed to have cut down our exports of rubber, we exported 5,000 tons direct to China and 3,800 tons to Hong Kong. These were official figures and

could not be and were not denied. Of course, as Admiral
Sherman of the U.S.A. said in a sworn statement of May
30th, 1951, which completely vindicated my whole position,
indirectly a great deal of other war material went to China
'by the use of ships flying foreign flags which went through
other ports'. Admiral Sherman gave specific examples.

The conduct of the Government became even worse when
the price of rubber was taken into account. At the start of
the Korean war the average price was 2s. per lb. It rose
month after month to a peak of 5s. 9d. in February 1951.
In the three months January, February and March 1951 on
the Government's own figures we sold 46,500 tons of rubber
to the Chinese who were fighting us in Korea at average
prices of 4s. 11d. in January, 5s. 9d. in February and 5s. 5d.
in March. In February the Prime Minister said: 'As regards
rubber I understand there is not a great amount going.'
Excluding indirect imports, rubber was then being exported
in volume twenty-two times as great as the year before.
Its monetary value was more than seventy times as much as
the year before. As I later said, 'The profit made out of this
war would make Sir Basil Zaharoff turn in his grave in
envy', and Sir Hartley Shawcross denied it, but the facts
showed that they were over £100,000,000 worth of exports.

Not one word was ever uttered by a Labour M.P. or
pacifist in support of the campaign to stop the export of war
materials to this country's enemies. Some Conservative
M.P.s were none too keen on the affair and I am sure that
more than one was on the receiving end of the profits.
In private most of my Labour friends treated me as well as
ever. Only a month or two before with all-party support I
had obtained a unanimous vote of the House for the first
reading of a Private Members' Bill to compel the football
pool promoters to publish their accounts. I am sure that the
majority of Labour Members felt no malice towards me.
They refrained from joining in the fray out of Party loyalty
and because a General Election was in the offing.

Surely this incident underlines two points: first, that
Ministers of the Crown can be staggeringly ignorant of
what is going on; secondly, that in the interests of the

country there should be some independent Members of
Parliament who cannot be gagged by Party loyalties. I
was never gagged by the Labour whips, with whom I was
very friendly. The pressure always came from some other
Labour Members who regarded criticism of the Government
in public as treason. The place for such criticism, they would
say, is in our private Party meetings. (I had tried it and found
it quite useless.) Their doctrine is, of course, essentially
totalitarian. In spite of all this I can only remember the
ordinary Labour Member of Parliament as a kindly,
generous, warmhearted and essentially lovable man.

CHAPTER XI

'Facilis Descensus'

BUT whatever my achievements may have been, my period in the House of Commons was marked by my progressive descent into alcoholism. At times I managed to stay without drink for a week or two. Strangely enough, I then felt not only much fitter but much happier. Moreover, my speeches were stronger and more effective. I believe it to be a popular illusion that a certain amount of drink is necessary to enable a man to be eloquent. It may be helpful in the case of intensely shy people—although the danger of their becoming addicted to alcohol must be taken into account. But people who want to speak are rarely shy, although they are frequently nervous. I do not believe that great debaters like Churchill and Bevan would be any the less effective if they were tee-totallers.

The causes of my drinking during this period lay very deep and I do not pretend to understand them fully. There is an old legal saying, 'The mind of man is not triable because the devil himself knoweth not the mind of man.' However that may be, it is certain that alcoholism is a progressive disease. It was so with me.

I did not even remain completely sober in the Chamber of the House of Commons itself. On four occasions I was to some extent under the influence of drink when I addressed the House. On one occasion, however, the matter had its somewhat humorous aspect.

Konai Zilliacus, the well-known left-wing Labour M.P., had taken a group of eight M.P.s, some of whom were suspected of being fellow-travellers, to the Soviet Union. They had been accorded a full-length interview with Stalin. Zilliacus on his return took the adjournment of the House of

Commons on Anglo-Soviet relations. Unfortunately for him the adjournment debate came on at four o'clock in the morning. The House had been debating a Bill at inordinate length and I had been refreshing myself at more than one of the seven bars in the House of Commons. I was passionately convinced that the march of the Soviet Union across the frontiers of the world should be halted before it was too late, that the best hope of peace was firmness and strength and loyalty to our American allies, and that those who believed America to be a war-monger were utterly wrong and likely, if taken seriously, to cause the very war they hoped to avoid. Moreover, to court the dictator who held millions in concentration camps, and even kept Buchenwald going as such a camp, seemed to me not only foolish but shameful.

I waited until Zilliacus had finished his speech and jumping to my feet asked Christopher Mayhew, the Minister who was to answer the debate, to give me a few minutes. He resumed his seat in my favour, being on friendly terms with me. I then attacked Zilliacus and his friends bitterly. They reacted with interruptions and taunts. 'Sit down', 'We want to hear the Minister', 'Crypto-Tory', and the like. Suddenly I said—or the gin said for me—'I have no intention of allowing the Minister to reply to those who advocate the appeasement of the Soviet Union. I propose to continue speaking until the debate is automatically adjourned as time is up.' There were loud protests and points of order, but I stuck to my decision and the Minister was unable to answer the debate.

On at least two occasions I made speeches which I would never have made if I had not been under the influence of drink. I was not, of course, drunk in the full sense of the word, but my powers of reasoning were affected.

A young man who believes that something of great value can be achieved by Membership of the House has the most intense disappointments waiting for him in that Palace of Frustration—even if he is successful in some ways. The kindly 'Georgie' miners' leader Will Lawther said to me, 'Politics is all right, Raymond, so long as you do not take it serious.' He was trying to warn me that a man must go with the Party machine and be content to be a small cog in it.

Of course a great deal of valuable information can be obtained through drinking with other Members and with visitors from all walks of life in the House. The bars are open as long as the House is open and I felt that I would be mean if I did not offer visitors a drink—which all too often led to a 'party'. But all this, although true, is not the real explanation of my heavy drinking. I drank to relieve my nervous tension. I was not drowning my sorrows. I went out to get drunk. I felt an almost irresistible urge to release the nervous tension within me. Again and again this urge came back, sometimes after I had done something which pleased me, sometimes after I thought that I had been unfairly prevented from achieving something.

An even more sinister habit than drinking in the House was drinking in afternoon clubs, in a wine bar in Fleet Street and later in night clubs. In these establishments I eventually came to spend almost £100 per week. Of course, that did not represent my own consumption only. An alcoholic rapidly collects around him a collection of the world's greatest spongers.

> 'When Raymond's in the lolly,
> The boys say "Let's be gay!"
> The boys say "Let's be jolly!"
> Well knowing who will pay.'

To which an R.A.F. friend of mine added later:

> 'Now Raymond's in the nick,
> There's gloom around the town,
> The drinks are not so quick,
> They have to buy their own!'

But the worst tricks of all are those that night-club owners and managers use to extract money from their customers when they are in their cups.

Personally I believe that the scandal of afternoon drinking clubs should be dealt with somehow. By paying five shillings, clubs are registered in dingy premises all over London, sometimes by people with long criminal records. Either we should have no licensing laws at all—there is a strong case for that on principle—or the licensing laws should be effectively enforced and should not be capable of being flouted and evaded so easily.

About this time I started to have occasional drinking bouts—which are the sure sign of an alcoholic. These might last two or three days with very little sleep intervening. A typical 'jag' of this kind might start quite innocently with a celebration with friends in Fleet Street. Suddenly I would become determined—or the champagne in me would determine—that I wanted to turn it into a real party. That would mean night clubs all night, adjourning after half past four in the morning to the pubs in Covent Garden, which open at that hour. Oscar Wilde wrote of the joy of seeing flowers arriving at dawn in the market. My joy was of a different variety—a game of darts, several pints of beer to get my second wind after all the champagne and spirits, and perhaps a song or two with a coloured singer whom we would have brought with us—subject to the permission of the landlord. Then about nine o'clock we might adjourn to an hotel, a club or even to a downstairs bar in the House of Commons, where I had a friend. And so the 'jag' would wear on until I reached the point of exhaustion.

Even today a man can drink legally in London for twenty-two hours out of twenty-four—and in practice even longer. The programme is as follows:

Public House	11 a.m.–3 p.m.
Afternoon Club	3 p.m.–5.30 p.m.
Public House	5.30 p.m.–11 p.m.
Night Club	11 p.m.–2.30 a.m.
Covent Garden Pub	4.30 a.m.–9 a.m.
Billingsgate Pub	9 a.m.–11 a.m.

This last experience of going from Covent Garden to Billingsgate to get in the extra drinking hour is the hallmark of an alcoholic.

Of course, during all this time I would meet sometimes the most extraordinary and interesting people. The men and women who come from night clubs to Covent Garden in the early hours of the morning to continue drinking comprise the most unlikely characters one would ever expect to meet, including even doctors, psychiatrists and famous experts on the human brain. No doubt if Shakespeare were alive, he would be seen there occasionally.

There was a set of people who used to frequent the Gargoyle Club (then under different management) whom I used mentally to classify as the Gaderene swine, because they seemed so obviously to be rushing at breakneck pace downhill. It is characteristic of the alcoholic that he may have insight into other people's affairs but not into his own. No doubt to many of the Gaderene swine I appeared to be one of them and they appeared to be interested spectators. Two of this set who attained fame and died of or through drink were Robert Newton, the film actor, and Dylan Thomas.

Dylan Thomas has, since his death and partly because of his early death, been accorded the laurels of immortality. I am sure that if his restless spirit surveys the scene of his posthumous triumphs, it smiles sardonically and has some very caustic comments on some of those who are now professed admirers. Dylan was undoubtedly an alcoholic and an excellent example of the principle which I have laid down that the alcoholic drinks either to relieve nervous tension or to ease a guilt complex. So guilty did he feel that he wrote to a friend: 'Weasels take off their hats as I stink by.' The nervous tension was obvious whenever one met Dylan the morning after—and an unexpected modesty and even shyness. Aneurin Bevan was a hero to him, belonging to a more substantial world than his world of the Sitwells.

Bob Newton was more difficult to assess from this point of view, but although it did not appear so much on the surface, the nervous tension was there. I saw it the day I tried to persuade him to have a drink in the Royal Court bar during one of his teetotal periods. I saw a glimpse of a soul in torment. He knew that drink would kill him, and he was making a last desperate effort to avoid his fate. His film contracts used to contain a clause by which he forfeited £1,000 every time he appeared drunk on the set.

I have never seen anyone so drunk as Newton used to get. One night he was having a terrible row with his wife Natalie (now dead), who was not frightened of him, but used to hit him hard over the head with her handbag. I went back with

EX

them to their flat. At the time Newton was playing the part
of Bill Sykes on the films and to a limited extent in real life.
In the flat he seized a bottle of gin and was about to hurl it at
Natalie when I restrained him. Eventually he was persuaded
to go. Natalie said she was frightened he might return and
asked me to stay the night. I could not very well refuse,
although there was only one bed. To my horror, an hour
later, I heard a car stop outside the flat and the very drunken
voice of Newton bawling at the driver. I was fairly well
dressed and sitting in a chair when he walked in. I felt very
nervous indeed. He paced up and down growling to himself,
'I smell evil; I smell evil.' Then the truth dawned on me.
He could not see me. Not long after, he went. Natalie was a
very tough girl, but this incident broke her down and she
cried, I am sure, out of genuine love for Bob. Looking back,
it seems incredible that I should have witnessed scenes like
this and continued on my alcoholic path, supremely confident that it could not happen to me.

I myself afterwards was sometimes in a condition not far
removed from that in which I then saw Robert Newton.
It is an awful experience and cannot be very far from
delirium tremens (which I have never suffered). I felt as
though my head was being pressed back by an unseen
irresistible force which always stopped just short of breaking
point. I was intensely restless and such sleep as I could
snatch was plagued by bad dreams. Above all, I felt in the
words put in Samson's mouth by Milton that 'I, a prisoner
myself, scarce freely draw the air imprisoned also'. If anyone
seriously doubts that alcoholism is a disease, let him explain
how any sane man after undergoing so terrible an ordeal
—worse than prison itself, as I know—could set his feet again
on the same path leading to the same fate. At the same time,
I am far from saying that for Robert Newton and Dylan
Thomas drink was not a necessary evil. Francis Thompson
asked in *The Hound of Heaven*, 'Ah must, Designer Infinite,
ah must Thou char the wood ere Thou canst limn with it?'
The answer in his case was that he killed himself with
laudanum, which was 10 per cent opium and 90 per cent
pure alcohol. The laudanum reduced him to sleeping on

the Embankment or under the arches, unless some unknown prostitute who had pity on him failed to find a customer for the night and took him home. Both Newton's acting and Thomas's poetry reached the heights when they were drinking very heavily.

Of the period after I left the House of Commons, of my divorce, my bankruptcy, my trial and conviction for offences of which I was in fact innocent, I do not wish to write at length. 'When sorrows come they come not single spies but in battalions.' Of all my sorrows the greatest by far was my divorce. Although not a Roman Catholic and indeed no more than an intellectual agnostic with a strong emotional longing to believe in a personal God, I am deeply opposed to divorce although not, of course, to legal separation. I believe that divorce on the whole has done immeasurably more harm than good. Lawyers get people who have lived and loved together for years to put down the most dreadful allegations against one another on paper. Thereafter reconcilliation becomes almost impossible. Sir Alan Herbert wrote an article one Sunday in which he wondered how many thousands of people had found happiness as a result of his Divorce Bill. But the same Sunday his own son-in-law, who had just divorced his daughter, wrote the saddest article I have ever read and characteristically referred to himself as 'the so-called innocent party'. They were my great friends and neighbours for many years and a source of joy to a host of people in addition to their charming children. I was in prison when I read these articles and the extraordinary contrast between them struck me very forcibly.

I do not now deny that my wife had very good reasons for divorcing me, although at the time I could not see it that way. I was getting drunk almost every day. A man in such a condition develops to a very high degree the Jekyll-and-Hyde characteristic. He is a completely different personality in drink. Even when sober he lacks insight into what is happening to him. He has frequent 'blackouts' so that he has no memory at all, or at best a hazy and inaccurate memory of what he has done. This not only increases his

guilt complex, but creates unjustified resentments. The only
solution of his troubles is to escape reality in drink, to live in
the past and to obtain for a few fleeting moments the exhilaration which comes with drunkenness. The road to hell
becomes broader and easier week after week. Perhaps if I
had not been born with a very strong constitution, I would
have been forced to stop drinking before I went to prison.
Even now I have not got an enlarged liver and there is nothing
wrong with me physically. Intellectually I have always
realised the immense dangers which are inseparable from
the possession of 'virtues' in the classical sense of the term.
But the abstract knowledge had no effect on my actions. If
only I had been born with a constitution which could not
withstand the appalling punishment which I inflicted on it,
life might have been much happier and more useful. In
prison I often pondered Milton's famous sonnet on his
blindness and sometimes thought I understood it. Now I find
it much more difficult to follow, but it surely contains at
least a hint that men should thank God for the afflictions as
well as the favours which nature has bestowed on them. So
often evil can lead to good and good to evil.

My memory of the years of my downfall is poor, although
I can remember most vividly what occurred before alcohol
had acquired its stranglehold on me. Mercifully the mind
tends to forget unpleasant and humiliating experiences. One
aspect of the treatment alcoholics receive from others
remains firmly fixed in my mind. Some people take advantage of them openly and brazenly. For instance, one day an
alcoholic friend of mine and I were short of money. 'I know
what to do', he said. ' "X" owes me fifty pounds and I
know that he is now fairly flush.' We went to see 'X' and my
friend asked him for the fifty pounds. 'No', said 'X'. 'Why?'
said my friend, expecting to hear 'X' deny that he had the
money and hoping to be able immediately to prove him a
liar. But 'X' said simply, 'Because you would only get drunk
with it. I am doing you a kindness by not paying it back.'
To this day 'X' has not repaid the money. I find it difficult
to accept that 'X' 's real reason for not paying the money
was the one he gave.

On three occasions I was charged with being drunk, and once with being drunk and disorderly. It is a fact not generally known that it is a criminal offence for a man to be drunk in a London street whether or not he is disorderly or interfering with passers-by. On the first occasion I was arrested by a young policeman when I was not drunk, but I pleaded guilty the next day to avoid the publicity. On the only occasion when I fought the charge of being drunk—because I was not frightened of the publicity—I was acquitted. The drill was to say to the magistrate only seven words: (Guilty?) 'Yes, sir.' (Anything to say?) 'No, sir.' (Fine of five shillings and doctor's fee.) 'Thank you, sir.' The first time I was convicted a note appeared in one or two papers without mentioning that I was an M.P. (The papers were not sure it was really myself that had been convicted.) The next day Brigadier Peto, M.P., whose brother I had defeated in the 1945 election, stopped me in the corridor and said, 'I thought you might be amused to see that there is another Raymond Blackburn.' I am glad that I told him the truth and also, as evidence of the sense of honour of most M.P.s, that I never heard that he had spoken to anyone else about it.

Although, as I have said, I was innocent of the offences of which I was convicted, my drinking habits led to personal carelessness which caused my downfall. I ceased to answer letters, and in legal cases if letters are produced and not answered they are generally believed, however wide of the truth they may be. I can understand how difficult it would be for anyone to believe that a solicitor would have been willing to act as informally as in fact I did.

As to the issue of my trial and conviction, I cannot write about it other than to say that it is still *sub judice*. It is, however, right that I should quote the following excerpts from two highly respected legal journals: *The Criminal Law Review* and *The Solicitors' Journal*.

The Criminal Law Review stated:
   '*Blackburn* was not referred to in the judgment of the Court of Criminal Appeal although it had been cited by counsel (Miss Rose Heilbron, Q.C.) in argument and she

had submitted (*The Times*, May 25, 1955) that if *Blackburn* was against her it was wrong. In his elaborate review of the matter Professor Glanville Williams also concludes that *Blackburn* was wrongly decided.'

The Solicitors' Journal stated:

'Here therefore is a decision of the Court of Criminal Appeal which appears to be wrong and to be bad law— on the authority of that same superior tribunal, as expressed in two appeals brought on the same issue shortly afterwards. On the other hand it is quite clear that the procedure adopted by Blackburn was wrong, however much he might have been wronged. The vital question arises: Is an aggrieved person powerless in such an awkward situation or are there effectual judicial proceedings available?'

CHAPTER XII

Wormwood Scrubs

As the heavy gates swung to behind me at Wormwood Scrubs at about seven o'clock on January 27th, 1955, I thought a little ruefully of the last time I had been there. I had been invited to lecture to three hundred prisoners in one of the prison blocks. Being very anxious not to 'talk down' to them, I had selected as my subject 'Some philosophical implications arising from modern developments in nuclear physics'. After a little while I had tried to enliven the lecture a little and I was astonished at the end by the acute and provocative questions from the prisoners. A little jokingly I had afterwards told many people that it was the best-looking and most intelligent audience I had ever addressed. Perhaps, I thought, I shall now find out how much I flattered them.

The prison officers in the Reception Department are pleasant and friendly people, and help to make up for the brusque manners of the junior Medical Officers. Moreover, there was one prisoner—an ex-lieutenant commander in the Navy—who was invaluable to the 'screws' and at the same time tried to help prisoners at this strange and forbidding outset of their prison careers. I was offered a cup of tea and some bread, and walked off to my cell. So far no one had given any sign that they had heard of me—although the evening papers carried headlines about my case for some time. When I arrived at 'C' prison block, however, a voice shouted at me from a cell, 'How much did you get?'

I replied, 'Two years'.

'Are you appealing?'

'Certainly.'

'Then you'll get five years, you —————— fool.'

After this I settled down to sleep, although I mistook the

bag containing my prison issue of toilet requisites for a pillow. I am a good sleeper and never remained awake all night throughout the entire period I was in prison. For the bad sleeper prison must be intolerable.

The following morning I saw the normal prison board—the Deputy Governor, the Chaplain and two others. They knew I was appealing against my conviction. Very few prison officers or Governors know that a man may appeal against conviction without appealing against sentence. It is, therefore, the habit of many prison officers to warn prisoners that if they appeal, they run the risk that their sentences may be increased. Just before my release I sought an interview with a Commissioner—R. D. Fairm, the Director of Prison Administration. I told him of this practice on the part of prison officers and even of Governors and Deputy Governors. He replied, 'But they are right in one sense. The chance might come up. It is like tossing a coin.' He did not know that a man may appeal against conviction without appealing against sentence. There is one sense in which even so an appellant is victimised. He loses forty-two or more days of the time during which he was an appellant except in rare cases, of which I was one. It may be that the confusion is caused by this rule.

I was put to work in the library. 'Work' is, of course, a euphemism for sitting about and either preparing unnecessary lists of books or occasionally scrubbing the floor. The library is a good 'number' and gave me the chance of reading *The Times*, and keeping abreast with events. My nearest fellow-worker in the library was a Harley Street surgeon of seventy-two, who was serving twelve months for abortion. Here I found the very opposite of the bitter middle-aged surgeon described in one of Galsworthy's short stories, *Late 399*. On the contrary, Dr 'X' did not complain of his sentence. 'I broke the law and I knew I was breaking it.' His only son had been killed as a bomber-pilot over Germany, but 'anyway it gives me the great pleasure of looking after my grandchildren'. Every morning he used to study the financial columns of *The Times*, to see how his very considerable shareholdings were currently valued. At the other end of the table was a Cockney whom he could not bear. The Cockney's worry was that he had no money and was soon 'going out'. Dr 'X' was a surtax payer on his investments alone. Yet here they were for a short space of time, equal in the sight of men as well as of God, and quarrelling with one another like children at school. Dr 'X' thought the Cockney was 'cheeky' (although I did not agree and often assured 'the Doc.' that it was mostly his own imagination). It would have meant nothing to 'the Doc.' to give the Cockney ten pounds, but it would have meant a great deal to the Cockney. Conversely, at the time it would have cost the Cockney nothing to be a little more respectful to 'the Doc.', who was a magnificent-looking gnarled old man straight out of a Rembrandt masterpiece.

'The Doc.' had a great sense of humour. He had indeed seen 'better days' and once had been consulted by the great Sir William Osler. He never complained, even when his fingers were blue with cold and he was in some danger of frost-bite. (February 1955 was the coldest February for many years.) One of his best remarks was about the difficulty of knowing the time in prison. Prisoners have no means of discovering the time for seventeen hours out of the twenty-four. 'Do you think', he asked me, 'that if a member of M.I.5. were in here, he could find out the time?'

The day after my arrival I met a former colleague of mine in the House of Commons, Peter Baker. He looked healthier than when I had last seen him, and some of his nervous mannerisms had gone. He was kind enough from time to time, as a 'red band' or trusty, to take me to the lavatory, which an ordinary prisoner cannot visit without official accompaniment. The Library Officer—a former sergeant-major—clearly enjoyed the prospect of having two former M.P.s and company commanders working under him. The Library Officer was a shrewd but kindly man. The advice he gave me was, 'Never make a friend in prison. Remember that if you really want a friend, a man like you will be better off with a screw as a friend than a con. Ninety-five per cent of the cons will let you down.' I had to leave the library in circumstances which I shall describe, but I am sure he was not responsible. There are many men in the prison service of excellent character and considerable ability. Why they joined the service is a mystery to me. Another example was Baker, an ordinary prison officer at Maidstone and a pre-war regimental sergeant-major. It is not pleasant to see these men condemned to a far longer term of imprisonment than the men they guard, and frustrated because the talent which they possess cannot be properly used.

'A man is not sent to prison for punishment, but as a punishment.' So runs the rule attributed to Sir Alexander Patterson. The comment was intended to mean that there should be no deliberate humiliation of a prisoner and that his life should not be made miserable by calculated measures. Such a formula suffers from the defect of being negative and not positive. Most prisoners in the south of the U.S.A. who had the choice preferred to have their legs permanently shackled and work on roads or in swamps rather than to be quiet and unmolested in a cell. Few men can bear their own company for long.

Wormwood Scrubs belongs to that class of prison to which men are sent pending their dispatch to the prison at which they are to serve the main part of their sentence. These prisons are known as local prisons, and prisoners spend there the first two or three months of their sentence, or perhaps even the first two years if they are undergoing a long sentence. Wormwood Scrubs is not regarded as a particularly strict prison. Most first offenders in the London area are sent to Wormwood Scrubs, but during my time there I met a few 'old lags'—generally up from Dartmoor for medical treatment. There are occasional lectures to the men, a film about once every three weeks, and in summer the men are even allowed on Saturday afternoon to play cricket with a tennis-ball. In spite of all this, the life of a prisoner in Wormwood Scrubs is very grim. I did not find it too unpleasant because I am a very good sleeper. I was occupied with my appeal, did quite a lot of writing and was happy to be able to read some books from the library which I had always been anxious to study—such as Trotsky's *Life of Stalin*. But to the average prisoner who is not particularly interested in books the long hours of confinement must be a torture.

In my block the men were called at 7.0 a.m. There were ten minutes for 'slopping out'—the process which has so often been described in which men queue up to empty their chamber-pots at the recesses, of which there are four per eighty-eight cells. A safety razor-blade is issued to each man for ten minutes and then collected again by a prison officer. (Each blade lasts ten days.) Breakfast of a pint of tea and a loaf of bread with margarine is handed to the prisoner and he is then locked in his cell. At about 9.10 he goes out to exercise, walking round the yard. This is the highlight of the day, as for half an hour in the morning and another half-hour in the afternoon he can stretch his legs and talk to the other prisoners whose company he likes. At 9.45 he goes to work. The rules as to talking at work are obscure. Apparently it is not an offence to talk at work, but a man can be put on a charge for refusing to obey an order, i.e. the order not to talk. This distinction is typical of the worst aspects of the prison system. In most 'shops' at Wormwood Scrubs a good deal of latitude is allowed by the officers, but there are a number of sadistic officers, as is to be expected, and they cause trouble from time to time.

At 11.30 the prisoner is marched back to his cell, picking up his 'dinner' on the way—of which the pint of soup is by far the most tasteful and nutritive part. He eats his 'dinner' alone in his cell, the door of which he bangs behind him. At 2.0 p.m. he is released again for half an hour's exercise, proceeds to work, returns to his cell at 4.30, and after tea, which is much the same as breakfast, is locked up again. At about 7.30 p.m. cocoa is served in his cell, but otherwise he remains locked up from 5.0 p.m. until 'slopping out' at 7.0 a.m. the next day. In short, during the three months I was at Wormwood Scrubs I was alone in my cell on weekdays for more than eighteen hours out of the twenty-four, and on Sundays for twenty hours. I found the long hours trying, but on the whole I did not mind the solitude. For other people with different temperaments and interests the confinement was obviously far worse agony than the hardest of hard labour would have been. Viewed as a punishment, prison is uneven in its effects. For the poor sleeper who is not fond of reading, prisons like Wormwood Scrubs must be unbelievably cruel.

Nothing surprised me more than the apparent composure —cheerfulness, almost—with which some prisoners who were first offenders started serving long sentences. There were three men, whose combined ages were nearly one hundred and eighty years, sentenced to a total of twenty-seven years between them. They had all held good positions in life—two of them were still quite well off. To a man of sixty a sentence of ten years might seem to have written 'finis' to the chapter of his life. But that was not their attitude. One of them— a retired regular major serving seven years for attempted murder of a girl who had taken most of his money—even said to me: 'You know, Blackburn, this enforced rest will put as many years on to my life as I spend in prison. I have not felt so fit for twenty years.' From what I learned after- wards, this sense of fitness was illusory. Men often leave prison looking and feeling fit and are dead within six months.

There is a sense of relief for many prisoners after the ordeal of prosecution and trial, even though they are convicted and receive severe sentences. Possibly in some cases it is because they feel that they have done something very wrong and that now by being sentenced they are paying their debt to society or to those they had wronged. In fact, of course, men in prison do nothing at all to help those they have wronged; they are not allowed, even where they would be able, to work especially hard so as to maintain their families or repay their debts. The feeling that in some strange way prisoners wipe the slate clean, as it were, by the very act of serving their sentence was accepted by Winston Churchill as Home Secretary, when he spoke of them on July 20th, 1910, as 'those who have paid their dues in the hard coinage of punishment'. No doubt it goes deep into the recesses of the human mind and is associated with the primitive belief that sacrifices of all kinds are pleasing to God. But it is utterly illogical and very far removed from reality. I know that even if I had been guilty, I should have done no one any good by going to prison. The only person who could possibly benefit from it would be myself, and to have rejoiced in the experience on that ground would be the height of selfishness. Moreover, morally no one is entitled to claim credit for something which happens to him through no wish of his own —which indeed in almost every case he has fought hard to prevent. Fortunately, perhaps, for them these views are not shared by the majority of prisoners. They agree with the youthful Winston Churchill.

The first weeks when a man is in prison are just the time when, if the Church of England had any real sense of its mission, it would do everything it could to ensure that he would reap the great advantages which can be derived from solitude—although compulsory solitude. I liked the Chaplain well—the Reverend Davies—and what I now write is in no way intended to be a reflection on him. He had about sixteen hundred men and boys in the prison to look after—and a parish on top of that. It would be farcical to suggest that he could have done his job properly even if he had had no parish responsibilities. The most he could do was to preach some excellent sermons, to welcome the occasional visiting choir, and to try to help a handful of prisoners.

The quality of the preacher who was frequently permitted to address us may be judged by the following piece, entitled *The Sermon*, which I wrote on the day on which it was delivered and managed to smuggle out of the prison the following day. Although it is intended to be funny, it actually happened just as I have described it:

THE SERMON

He was an earnest, bespectacled little man with a blank, humourless face and the accent of a 'boy made good' from Staffordshire. I am sure that he had thought long and hard about the sermon he would deliver to those hundreds of men in the suits of shabby grey. He took his cue from the Deputy Governor, who had read in a firm, factual voice, Revelations XXI: *And I saw the holy city, new Jerusalem coming down out of heaven from God, made ready as a bride adorned for her husband.*

Unfortunately, after some of the most beautiful lines ever written, this chapter gets bogged down in a mass of detail. *The first foundation was jasper; the second sapphire; the third chalcedony; the fourth emerald; the fifth sardonyx*—and so forth.

It was the detailed information about the new Jerusalem which fascinated our practical preacher.

But first he dealt a left and a right at his theoretical enemies. The left was to our over-credulous brethren the British Israelites, who, he said, believe that the future can be foretold from a close examination of the Book of Revelations. This was an error. But far worse was the error of those who scoffed at the vision and even suggested that the details were quite fanciful.

The preacher paused for so long that everyone must have fixed their eyes on him. Dramatically he plunged *in medias res*.

'Some of us', he said, 'have fallen by the wayside.' Somehow he did not look as if he had fallen by the wayside himself, and we gathered that he was not referring to the Deputy Governor. 'But', he went on, 'there is hope even for those who have fallen by the wayside.' He invited us to consider verse 16 of Revelations XXI, which proves it: *And the city lies foursquare and the length thereof is as great as the breadth; and he measured the city with the reed, twelve thousand furlongs; the length and the breadth and the height thereof are equal.* 'Think of London', he said, 'and then think of this enormous city one thousand five hundred miles square.' (My mind unconsciously tried to work it out. The answer is 2,250,000 square miles and 3,375,000,000 cubic miles.) 'Draw a line on a map', he said, 'between London and Moscow. Then draw another line parallel to that but fifteen hundred miles to the south. Think of it. The whole of the area between those lines corresponds to the area covered by the Eternal City. So, you see, there must be room for all who believe and win through, even for those who have fallen by the wayside. Why', he cried, 'the southern line would go through Benghazi.' An Eighth Army veteran behind me cannot have been following the drift of the argument. 'Benghazi can be as hot as hell', he opined.

The preacher made his main point at some length. But

he had two other verses up his sleeve, of which one at least
was even more apposite to our situation.

First, verse 23: *And the city hath no need of the sun neither of the
moon to shine upon it; for the glory of God did lighten it and the light
thereof is the Lamb.* 'This means that it is always day. There is
always light. There are no secrets. Everyone can always
see what everyone else is doing.' The 'snout' smuggler on
my right looked very uneasy. I thought rather wildly of a
hideous dream I had of a world in which the scientists had
improved television to the point where one could switch on a
set and have a look at any time of the day or night at anyone
else one wished, whatever he or she might be doing. Some of
the hideous dreams of our fathers are the realities of today. . . .
But concentrating again on the preacher, I could see that his
thoughts turned in an entirely different direction. His point
was that in the Eternal City we criminals could not get into
trouble again. 'Nothing can go wrong when everyone knows
what everyone else is doing.' The logic was irrefutable. In
such a City there cannot be cheats because cheating is
impossible. Even if some of our friends were to try a bit of
cheating to keep their hand in, it would of course only be a
matter for tolerant amusement.

But the best was yet to come. There is only one gate in a
prison—the same gate at which one enters it, and leaves it
—unless one has an appointment with Pierrepoint. The
Eternal City has twelve gates. *On the east were three gates and on
the north three gates; and on the south three gates; and on the west
three gates . . . and the twelve gates were pearl gates.*

Now the measurements of the city and the wall are given
in the chapter, but for some strange reason not the measurements of the gates, although *he that spake with me had for a
measure a golden reed to measure the city and the gates thereof.*
I have read the chapter again and again and can find no
warrant for the preacher's assertion: 'Every gate is seventy-
two yards wide.' I know that my ears did not fail me because
several of us discussed the matter while on exercise the same
afternoon, and we all agreed that we had distinctly heard the
preacher give us this information—presumably from his own
private revelation.

But he was working up to a great climax. There was a final triumphant burst of ecstasy in his praise of 'the City on the Other Side' as a paradise for prisoners. 'You need not fear to enter the City. You can go in through the gates and out through the gates as and when you please throughout the whole twenty-four hours of the day. Read verse twenty-five. *And the gates thereof shall in no wise be shut by day (for there shall be no night there).*'

That afternoon, as we paced the prison yard, one of my colleagues referred to one phrase in the sermon which had disconcerted him. The preacher had, of course, spoken with admiration about the wall of the City, *a hundred and forty-four cubits according to the measure of man, that is, of an angel*. What, we wondered, was the purpose of the wall? Then we remembered that our preacher had answered this question: 'To keep out undesirable characters', he had said cryptically. We looked at one another in consternation. Could not this one remark, broadly interpreted, nullify the effect of the whole sermon, so far as we were concerned?

But worse was to come. The very next Sunday the same preacher was in the pulpit and evidently something had seriously disturbed him. Instead of announcing a text, he said that he would talk about something he had recently found written by a prisoner in his cell: 'Crime pays'. When he had asked the prisoner what the words were meant to convey, the prisoner replied, 'I've got plenty of money stashed away and I'm looking forward to a hell of a good time when I get out.' Instead of regarding this as the futile and probably mendacious boast which it was, our preacher had allowed it to infuriate him, and now proceeded to vent his fury on us. He said that we must distinguish between the interim dividends from crime and the final dividends. No doubt the interim dividends might be pleasant, but they would always be out-weighed by the final dividends. 'Think', he said, 'of the deterioration that takes place in prison and think of the agony of the loved ones of the prisoner outside.' At that I stepped out from the pew where I was sitting and shouted in my anger some such words as, 'This is intolerable. I will not listen to this maniac.'

I turned round as a couple of officers came up to me and I glared at the Governor in the organ-loft. The preacher stopped speaking. I walked out of the chapel, followed by an officer who took me back to my cell. 'Feeling ill?' he said, intending to be helpful. But I was not willing to accept that get-out. 'Certainly not', I said. 'If I had stayed I should have prevented that idiot from finishing his sermon.' The officer said, 'A lot of us have thought that it was high time something was done about him. I don't suppose that they will charge you.' Nor did 'they', but the next day I was removed from the library and sent to work in the tailor's shop.

At the tailor's shop I soon made friends with two instructors who really did their best to make life as pleasant as possible for the prisoners. They would argue heatedly about politics with one another—one was Labour and the other Conservative. I used to amuse myself by providing both of them with arguments and then watch them hammer away at one another with every appearance of intense conviction. They were both firm friends but really hated one another's politics. Of course, it is easier for 'instructor' officers to get on with prisoners than for discipline officers. Indeed, sometimes while we were having fun together, I would see the discipline officer in the hut looking furious because he could not restrain us. Some 'screws' think that a prisoner should never smile, let alone laugh. One or two even thought that I was trying to be sarcastic when I said, 'Good morning, sir.'

The reasons for the attitude of some of the 'screws' became plainer to me one day when I went out by special permission to see my solicitor and Sir Frank Soskice, who most generously offered to help me over my appeal, and refused to take any fee. I was accompanied by two officers. To my astonishment one was a young man with whom I had had a row in the bath-house. I had thought him almost insane and wondered why just before I was due to leave for the day out he came to me and said, 'Please forget about what happened the other day. I have had a bad accident with a motor-cycle and I get fearful headaches. Will you please accept my apology?' I said, 'Certainly. I have forgotten all about it.'

In the taxi, he said, 'Do you know what the cons think of

us screws? They regard us as the scum of the earth, lower
than they are themselves. And so do most people round here.
I even hate going into my tobacconist, because he is always
cracking the same horrible joke. He says, "So they let you
out again", and everyone in the shop looks at me in horror.'
No doubt this officer—whom I came to like despite our first
contretemps—was exaggerating. But the experienced principal officer who was with us agreed with him. The bad
feeling between officers and men is a two-way traffic.
They return the hatred or contempt that they assume to exist
on the other side.

There is one aspect of a prisoner's life at Wormwood
Scrubs which is an absolute disgrace to the prison system and
which the Commissioners know about and do nothing to
remedy—namely, the conditions under which visits take
place. A prisoner is ordinarily entitled to one visit of half an
hour every month. That is not a long time, even if the conditions for a visit were ideal. There must obviously be many
things which a man does not wish to put in a prison letter.
(He is allowed one letter per fortnight and every letter is
censored.) The hut in which the ordinary visits take place
is dark and often dirty. The prisoner is separated from
his visitor by a long wooden partition in which there are
windows covered with wire netting through which he is supposed to talk. It is very difficult to hear and almost impossible
to see in such conditions. One would have thought that the
Commissioners would have had sufficient pride not to inflict
such discomfort and even humiliation on people who are only
performing a recognised Christian duty in visiting prisoners.
No doubt, the absurd defence would be put up that to make
conditions for visits tolerable would be to increase the risk of
'smuggling'. But that could easily be prevented by giving
every prisoner a 'dry bath' before and after the visit; that is
by stripping and searching him. Shortage of prison officers
is no excuse as during the afternoon there are plenty of
officers who could be spared.

I had visits in connection with my appeal, and as my most
frequent visitor was accredited officially as a clerk to my
solicitor, the visits were in one or other of the two rooms set

aside for solicitors and counsel. Even so, in the bitter weather
of February one of the rooms was always without a fire and
was bitterly cold. The Governor and the Governor's Clerk
did everything they could to help me, but as the Governor's
Clerk said to me, conditions in Wormwood Scrubs are quite
unsuitable for a man who is conducting an appeal in a
complicated case.

Although Wormwood Scrubs is the prison to which first
offenders go, there are a considerable number of men there
who have had two or three convictions, and have become
hardened criminals. It seems very wrong that they should be
mixed up with young boys like one I met who I am convinced was innocent, and anyway was obviously the reverse of
a criminal type. The Commissioners constantly talk about
the need for segregating the worst types of prisoner from the
young men who are in prison for the first time. All they have
to do is to visit Wormwood Scrubs and other prisons themselves and talk to twenty men at random and they will
discover how utterly unfounded is the claim that this is being
done. There should be a separate local prison in the London
area, or at least a separate wing of a prison where youthful
offenders can be sent with the certainty that they will meet
no other prisoners who will corrupt them; of course, this
would be useless if they were afterwards sent to prisons like
Maidstone where nearly a third of the men are undergoing
corrective training, that is, have at least three convictions
behind them. The whole subject of first offenders—particularly the young ones—is in need of urgent attention.
No doubt, if the Bishop of London had bothered to visit
Wormwood Scrubs instead of lunching with the Judges at the
Old Bailey, something might have been done even in
January 1955. As it is, so far as they or I could see, no one
knew or cared what happened to the young men who were
with me in the Scrubs. No doubt, at Maidstone or the Verne
or wherever they went, some trouble would be taken with
them. But by that time much of the possible damage had
been done.

CHAPTER XIII

Maidstone

MAIDSTONE, when I went there, still enjoyed the reputation of being Britain's showpiece as a prison. This was almost entirely due to a remarkable man—John Vidler, the Governor. His Chaplain, John Nicholls, had been a great help to him and took a great deal of care over finding accommodation for outgoing prisoners as well as entertainment for the prison. But it is the Governor who sets the tone of a prison, and insofar as Maidstone was a better prison than any other, it was to John Vidler that the real credit was due.

When I arrived at Maidstone, he was already in poor health, although he could still play an occasional game of golf. He had been a triple blue at Oxford—rugger, cricket and golf—and had played cricket for Sussex. I was a little astonished to find a Governor wearing a blazer and flannels and having an unmistakably mad look in his eyes. I have no doubt he required to be a bit mad to make any impression at all on the dull officialdom of the prison system. One day I mentioned the Commissioners to him and he said, 'The Commissioners? If I had my way I would have them flogged', and he sounded as though he meant it. Only by developing a very thick hide for the constant pricks and reprimands of the Commissioners and the Home Office was he able to introduce a measure of humanity into prison routine. Just before he left, he said to me, 'You can quote me on this. I have analysed over a thousand cases of men as exhaustively as I could. I believe I know as much about the causes of crime—certainly I ought to—as any man alive. And I know nothing. Without understanding the cause of a disease, one is in the dark in prescribing treatment. One thing and one thing only I claim to have done, and I know it has helped. A man in prison must break his heart. I have seen to it that he did not break his heart against the brick wall of officialdom. That way lies hopeless bitterness.'

My first meeting with him was not altogether fortunate. He was the chairman of the Reception Committee when I arrived. First, looking at my record, he expressed astonishment that it was possible for a person to get drunk on the liquor now sold in Britain. I bore this with composure. Then he attacked me with the following question: 'Have you a sense of humour?' A newly-arrived prisoner is not particularly anxious to score off the Governor, but this put me in an impossible situation. I replied, 'People whom I have met who pride themselves on their sense of humour, usually possess none.' He acknowledged the justice of this remark.

John Vidler sent me to a block whose Assistant Governor was a former Lecturer in Philosophy in the University of Wales, named Gordon Hawkins, with whom I was able to strike up a friendship. If there is one place where one should try to acquire a philosophic mind it is prison. Unfortunately Hawkins belonged to the school of the logical positivists, than whom nothing more negative can be imagined. But it was a great pleasure to talk to a highly intelligent man. He was an ardent admirer of John Vidler—although he was never able to extract from Vidler any explanation of the principles on which he had become so excellent a Governor. Hawkins believed that people in prison were very much the same as people outside prison—only they had been unfortunate either through lack of money or through women (whom he asserted to be at the bottom of the majority of cases). We had a number of utter villains in the block. His views were really a curious combination of charity and cynicism—it pleased him that he could really claim that he treated prisoners as human beings at the same time as it tickled some imp in his brain to say that they were no better and no worse than an average cross-section of humanity.

A great deal has been written about the so-called 'Maidstone system'. There was really no such thing. Four hundred prisoners were kept in a circular area with a diameter of about four hundred yards. Their sentences were generally between two and four years—which with remission meant that prisoners spent more than one and less than three years in Maidstone. Remission is one third of a man's sentence—unless he is serving preventive detention. The good things about Maidstone were the following:

(1) The prisoners with really bad records knew that the Governor was personally concerned about their individual cases. I have heard him abuse men at the top of his voice, his face suffused with fury. He knew that by so doing he was putting it out of his own power to punish them for the offence they had committed. His conduct would have shocked the Commissioners—and indeed almost anyone—and it was certainly offensive to prisoners like myself who witnessed it. But it was the measure of the man's deep anxiety to save anyone under his care from a life of crime, that he counted his own dignity as of no importance.

(2) The prisoners were kept out of their cells from early morning until 7.30 p.m. at night. They were allowed to have their lights on until 10 p.m.—one hour later than Wormwood Scrubs and other prisons where the rules as to lights being put out at 9 p.m. and kept out until 6.30 the next morning appear designed to ensure that a man is awake a long time in the dark in a small cell. There were, of course, disadvantages in this system for men like myself who thought that at least silence and solitude could be found in prison— and instead had to listen to the most infernal noises from the wireless and our fellow prisoners even if we retired to our cells. But the young prisoners must have benefited by being kept out of their cells where they would have been utterly bored and grown bitter.

(3) It was generally known that if a charge was brought against a prisoner, the Governor would consider the evidence fairly and without the usual prejudice in favour of his prison officers. This was not popular with the 'screws' themselves. They would from this point of view have preferred the régime of a well-known Governor who said once to a prisoner, 'If any of my officers told me that he found a

prisoner riding round the second landing on a bicycle, I should believe him.' There were few petty charges at Maidstone, with good results for staff and prisoners alike. As in the Army, so in prison, nothing causes more irritation and unpleasantness than the exaggeration of unimportant incidents by men in conditions of subordinate authority who love to display their power over people under them.

(4) Under Vidler a great effort was made in the case of many prisoners to find accommodation for them when they left, and also to find jobs for them. He was well-liked in Maidstone and local employers used to help him. This was a great service for the benefit of the prisoners concerned and helped to improve the morale of the prison.

(5) Vidler gave more responsibility to 'blue bands', or trusties, than is usual. Indeed, a number of them thought they were running the prison. He chose for advancement a considerable number of young men of bad character in the hope that the trust imposed in them would have some effect. In this he was generally unsuccessful and aroused the hostility of a number of elderly prisoners of good character as a result. But it was an experiment well worth trying, even though, as I think, it was a failure. The main reason it failed is that the young men concerned, instead of accepting the trust as a sign that there was goodwill for them, believed that they had been very smart in persuading the authorities to give them positions of which they could take advantage.

But great as all these achievements may appear to have been, they count for little beside the facts that most of the men in the prison were engaged in false or futile work— the exact words being not mine but those of an Assistant Governor—and that when they came out of prison, they could not be given more than two or three pounds.

The question of work lies at the root of the prison problem. Most of the real criminals are men who have descended into a life of crime through an abhorrence of hard work. Prison should form in them the habit of hard work and in the process they should be taught to save. The ideal form of hard work for prisoners is work on the land or on public projects such as road-making. In the United States of America prisoners preferred to be shackled and set to work in gangs rather than to stay shut up in local prisons. There are large areas in this country, such as those near the Romney marshes, where land now lies useless and could be reclaimed with great advantage to the country. Every pound's worth of agricultural produce which prisoners could obtain from such land would not only be a source of great satisfaction to the prison authorities but would directly improve our balance of payments position. Contrary to popular impression, prison labour is eagerly sought after by farmers who find that by distributing a few packets of cigarettes they can get more reliable and harder work than from most agricultural labourers. And by requisitioning land now derelict, the Commissioners could establish a number of prison camps in which they could give direct proof of the value of prison labour.

One of the Assistant Governors at Maidstone, a former Group Captain in the R.A.F., had been the Governor of Aldington Camp, the prison camp attached to Maidstone. There he had made a large profit for the Commissioners with the labour of about seventy or eighty prisoners who were taken to work in gangs by lorries and hired out to local farmers at about £7 or £8 per week. He told me that complaints from the farmers were very unusual; indeed, that the main complaint was that there was not more labour of this kind. The food at Aldington Camp, although better than at Maidstone, was inadequate in protein content for really hard work—which makes the record of these prisoners all the more impressive.

It is astounding to me that Home Secretaries ignore the obvious fact that most prisoners suffer from bugs in the brain of some sort. (If they do not suffer from them before they go to Wormwood Scrubs or Wandsworth, they will soon enough after their arrival.) The effect of keeping such men packed together in a confined space can only be to pack the bugs tighter. What is needed is fresh wind and open air and hard work to clean their minds and make their bodies fit.

My own work at Maidstone was done in the front stores,

the garden party, the Methodist Chapel, the synagogue and the library.

My first job was in the front stores. With another prisoner I would lift up the two heavy milk churns at the front gate and deliver them to the kitchen. I necessarily had to deliver the milk to prisoners at the other end. At first I found that there were four or five prisoners waiting at the kitchen with mugs to dip into the milk, so that it was obvious to me that a good deal of the milk was stolen before being put into use. My companion also helped himself. For the first three or four days I pretended not to notice, but then I decided that I would put a stop to it. Stealing from a comrade in the Army is regarded as a very serious matter and so should stealing from comrades be regarded in prison. When I spoke to the civilian in charge of the stores, he told me that he did not want to know about it and that the Governor discouraged minor matters becoming the subject of complaint by officers or the civilian staff.

I then said to my companion: 'From now onwards I am going to deliver this milk under the eye of the officer and we will go right past the hangers-on, and nobody, including yourself, will take any milk.' He said: 'You are not going to "grass", are you?' I replied: 'It is not a question of grassing. There is no grassing in my telling you what is going to be done, and if I am impeded in doing what I want, a row will develop which would no doubt bring officers in. In any event, I am not concerned with the ridiculous codes about grassing.' We delivered the milk together. The usual three or four prisoners were waiting and were surprised at the grim faces of the men carting the milk churns past them and delivering them on the floor. Afterwards I had no more trouble, although my companion said that he had had to do the people concerned some other favour in order that we might remain on friendly terms.

Not long afterwards, I was alone in his office with the Governor, John Vidler, and with Jimmy Good, his clerk. They prided themselves on the fact that through informers they got to know whatever happened in the prison within twenty-four hours. They both knew that I was getting on

F

quite well with the prisoners generally, but John Vidler used to like to pull my leg. He had obviously had some account of this incident because he said something like: 'Why, you are even having a row with the boys in the' kitchen.' I then said to him, 'I want your word that no disciplinary action of any kind will be taken as a result of my telling you about it, without mentioning any names.' He gave me his word and I told him the story. He replied, 'I don't approve of this but, of course, a certain amount of fiddling in prison is inevitable, as it is in the Army.' I said, 'Well, whatever you think you may do to me in prison, you are not going to turn me into a thief.'

In fact, a certain amount of petty pilfering of this kind is inevitable and a great deal takes place in relation to food. In my view, a very much stricter system for the supervision of food supplies is required in all prisons. It is surely absurd that, if a prisoner is to be issued with one sheet of paper, he has to go through a tremendous rigmarole and it has to be entered on his record, but that valuable food should constantly go astray through no proper check being kept upon it.

My job in the front stores was considered a good one, but there was really very little work to do. If any visiting official came round, the civilian in charge would ask me to manage to look busy, if I could. He was a former petty officer in the Navy and a decent enough man. He had, however, something approaching a mania about the need to keep people out of the stores and to issue the very minimum of stores required. If thirty new prison officer's hats came in, he would hope to be able to keep three or four on the side somewhere, unknown to anybody else. There was absolutely no wrongful motive behind his actions, but he simply hated to part with what he had—unless it was merely routine. One day I let a senior prison officer into the stores, while the ex-petty officer was out, to try on a hat which had been delivered for him. I did not allow him—if 'allow' is the right word—to take the hat away, I merely let him try it on. This sent my 'boss' into a transport of fury as a result of which I was transferred by the Governor—who knew about the facts—to a better job on the garden party, which kept me in the open during the glorious summer of 1955.

A job on the garden party is really the best work in the prison (except during the winter). There is only one serious drawback and that is the Garden Party Officer, described by Commander Heckstall-Smith, D.S.C., as 'the most foul-mouthed, nasty officer in the whole prison'.

This officer is a wizened old man with a very definite grudge against so-called 'gentlemen'. Having been so attacked by Heckstall-Smith, I felt that he might be forgiven for regarding me, another possible writer, with great sus-picion and even hostility. He did so. But for quite a long time I managed to get on fairly well with him—although he kept my pay at below 2s. per week, however hard I worked. The first time he crawled towards me, I was attempting to hoe. He said, 'It doesn't matter 'oo you are or where you come from. You can't 'oe back. You must 'oe forward.' I found his advice to be sound. Sometimes he became very disconsolate. One day we were squashing caterpillars—he insisted on my doing it with bare fingers—when I said, 'I wonder what use caterpillars are'. He replied, 'No ——— use, like me.' I tried to comfort him, telling him, as was true, that his gardens were a joy to behold, and that by providing so wonderful a display of flowers, he was serving his fellow-men. He grunted, but I believe he was pleased.

Unfortunately, after three months, the inevitable major row developed—owing to his stupidity rather than to any malice on his part. The Chief Officer sent a message over to the gardening officer to say that the outside lavatories needed cleaning and requesting him to detail two men to do so. By chance I was near the conservatory which was Marsh's normal headquarters, and to my astonishment he detailed me for the job of cleaning the outside lavatories and placed me under the supervision of an old coloured prisoner named Johnson, who was in fact an exceedingly nice man but more or less incomprehensible. Johnson was, of course, very embarrassed at having me placed under his orders to clean outside lavatories. I said, 'I don't know how to clean lavatories—perhaps you would be good enough to show me yourself.' The old man gave me a look and then proceeded to give an exhibition. He is a very obstinate old man. However, after he went away, I cleaned two or three lavatories and then decided that it really was not good enough. I went over to see the Principal Officer on duty and as soon as he heard what the gardening officer had done, he said, 'The old ———. He is really quite off his rocker. I will tell him straight away that you are not to be put on work of that kind.' It was by now about lunch-time. Yet after lunch when the gardening officer returned, he still continued to detail me for the work. I therefore said, 'Sir, I wish you to know that I propose to report your conduct to the Governor and inform him of your disobedience of orders.' He then said, 'Are you refusing work?' (which is, of course, a crime). I said, 'No, I am reporting you to the Governor.' We then walked over together to the centre where he tried to persuade the Principal Officer then on duty to have me 'banged up'. That Principal Officer said, however, that I was entirely within my rights to complain to the Governor and that I had better return to my usual work pending an enquiry into the matter. The officer had, of course, disobeyed orders and, on my complaint, although not in my presence, was very severely rebuked by the Deputy Governor. The Deputy Governor told me that he had left him under no illusions whatever as to the very serious view which he took of his disobedience. Nevertheless, he said that it was in my interests not to stay on the garden party.

That is how I came to be, of all things, the Synagogue and Methodist Chapel cleaner.

Afterwards, the old man used to say about me—and I do not think he really disliked me—'I've 'eard of you ——— grassing one another, but 'e grassed *me*.'

Incidentally, at the end of the front lawn, the murderers are buried, including George Joseph Smith, the Brides in the Bath murderer. There is nothing to mark their graves, and sometimes odd bones come up.

During his short sojourn in Maidstone awaiting execution, Smith's hair turned white and, in the opinion of the then Chaplain and of his Bishop, he became a saint. Although admitting his many crimes involving fraud and bigamy, he maintained to the last his innocence of murder and said that the deaths of his three wives by drowning in their baths were pure coincidence.

During the first six months of my stay at Maidstone, my relationship with other prisoners fluctuated a good deal as a result of the way in which I treated the officers. The relationship between most officers and most prisoners is one of hostility and even contempt. Maidstone was undoubtedly an exceptional prison in that a few prison officers were even liked by a considerable number of prisoners. But beneath the surface the suspicions were there. I adopted the attitude that I would be equally friendly with officers and prisoners, and as a result, established after a time a satisfactory relationship with both. But at first the fact that I would be seen talking to and joking with officers at various times caused trouble. To their credit the officers themselves warned me that this might occur. One day I was the last to queue up for soup and the men behind the canteen so arranged it that there was none for me. Their 'blue band' and the chief instigator of the trouble was a big Irishman named Stewart who was serving a sentence for manslaughter and was a violent character. When I reached my table and found that they were jeering at me, I was most annoyed, particularly as I had done nothing to excite such discrimination. I walked angrily up to the bar of the canteen and, pointing at Stewart, denounced him to an officer. A fight between Stewart and myself very nearly developed then and there. When I went back to my table I was hissed by most of the men in the hall. I shouted back at them. They knew perfectly well that Stewart and his associates had for some time discriminated in favour of their friends and against those they disliked in dishing out the food. But they thought that one should tamely submit to it rather than have a row in the presence of a 'screw'. For some time after this I was hissed wherever I went in the prison. Although amused, I thought it better to ignore it. In the course of time opinion swung in my favour as the dining-hall staff were changed and the new men were more courteous as well as fairer than the old.

The extraordinary fact was that more than one of these men who accused me of being a 'grass' were really themselves 'grasses'. This is apparently quite frequent and many cases of violence result from false allegations of 'grassing' being bandied about by the very people who were themselves responsible. The system whereby Prison Governors rely on informers who are permitted to remain anonymous—sometimes even to catch out prison officers—is most reprehensible. If a very serious offence is involved—such as razor-slashing—the use of informers of this sort is permissible. But where, as is most usual, the information relates to smuggling of tobacco, it should be beneath the dignity of a Governor to make use of it—unless the informer insists upon being personally and openly responsible for the charge. Very extensive use of informers was made at Maidstone, according to John Vidler himself, who said that the trouble was that he could not obtain authentic and advance knowledge of what was going on by any other means. Obviously he had felt the greatest distaste in the beginning for having to use informers. Unwholesome practices can appear to become justifiable when used as part of a routine.

An enormous amount has been written about 'snout' smuggling and the 'snout Barons'—the men who lend tobacco at 50 per cent interest per week. Undoubtedly a great deal of the trouble in prison is the result of the lending of tobacco and the methods which are used to compel borrowers to pay. While I was at Maidstone a young fair-haired lad received a razor-slash from the top to the bottom of his cheek, measuring at least five inches. He had to be taken to a civilian hospital. His explanation of the injury was quite absurd—that he had cut his cheek accidentally through having a safety razor-blade mixed up with his towel. In the end the Governor accepted this explanation and treated the case as closed. I resolved to find out the truth and some four months afterwards managed to do so. The motive was tobacco. 'Jackie' had borrowed a great deal of tobacco and failed to repay it after many warnings. His assailant was a 'blue band', one of the men selected by the Governor for promotion from the ranks. Although 'Jackie' did not approve

of the method of redress used against him, he was not willing
to give any information about his attacker, who got off scot
free. I have since heard that he has returned to prison with a
sentence of five years.

CHAPTER XIV

Some Prisoners I Have Met

IN the course of my prison experiences I met an extra-ordinary variety of prisoners, ranging from murderers whose crimes shocked millions of people to insignificant and half-witted individuals who seemed to me utterly incapable of forming any criminal intent. It is wrong that young impressionable first offenders should be brought into close contact with the worst criminals, but for my part I found it very interesting.

Murderers are in a category of their own. Reprieved murderers are notoriously good prisoners, and judging by my knowledge of two men named Hepper and Wells, the same can be said of murderers who are not reprieved. The saying, 'There but for the grace of God go I', appears to apply even more to murderers than to any other class of criminal. It seems that, given the maximum temptation, a normal man is more inclined to kill his fellow man or woman than, say, to forge his signature. Many murderers, of course, are also confirmed criminals, but it seems that in committing murder they break, as it were, the crime barrier.

It is a question whether any man can commit murder without losing possession of his reason to such an extent as to be insane, in the popular sense of the word. A psychiatrist addressing the Prison Chaplains in 1955 told of the case of a man who cut off the hands of his own child and left them on his wife's plate for breakfast. Yet, he said, the man was not insane. This extraordinary remark well illustrates the confusion surrounding the whole subject of crime and insanity. My godfather, Professor Charles Mercier, a famous penologist, said proudly on his deathbed, 'I have taught that insanity is a disease of conduct'. The fact is, however, that unless and until we reach the stage when organic disease of the brain cells can be proved in such cases, it is a matter of opinion whether such conduct as that of the father in question, or of Hepper who raped an eleven-year old girl, or of D., who killed his own daughter in a frenzy of rage because her mother had committed adultery, is compatible with sanity. The law required only that the prisoner should be suffering from such a disease of the mind that he did not understand the nature and quality of his act or, if he did, that he did not know it was wrong—not wrong morally but wrong according to the law. The medical experts testified their opinions one against the other. In the case of D., whom I knew very well while awaiting trial, Dr Mathieson and other experts believed him sane but the jury found him insane. So far as I could see he was perfectly sane, but nevertheless I agree with the verdict of the jury because such conduct appears to me to be incompatible with sanity.

Hepper's was a very interesting case because he appeared —and I believe genuinely was—absolutely convinced of his innocence. The issue of insanity was confused and in the result he was hanged—an end which he undoubtedly feared.

Hepper was a sixty-three year old artist who had been extradited from Spain on a charge of murdering an eleven-year-old girl in Brighton. Like almost all prisoners, he had the regrettable habit of talking about his own case for far longer than one really wished to listen. But on many subjects he was most interesting. He was a Gibraltarian, born on the Rock itself, with a melancholy ascetic face. He spoke English with a pronounced Spanish accent and although a British subject clearly was more Spanish than British in temperament. Indeed, he possessed Spanish nationality and bitterly criticised General Franco for having agreed to his extradition. This, he said, was due to his strong Republican sympathies. He had fought against the Falangists in Galicia in the North-West of Spain, and had brought volunteers from Portugal to fight against Franco. In Portugal he had for twelve years been Counsellor at the American Legation and claimed also to have engaged in espionage against both Salazar and Franco. All this he believed to be recorded against him in the official file concerning him in Madrid, with the result that the Spanish authorities agreed to the extradition of a man who had Spanish as well as British nationality.

The Spanish prisons, he said, were quite revolting. 'This place is a palace compared with them. The food is atrocious and there is terrible overcrowding.' (Unfortunately the overcrowding in British prisons today is quite bad enough.) But Hepper and his fellow-artists were allowed one great privilege in the Spanish prison. They could sell their paintings or other works of art and receive half the proceeds of the sale, the other half going to the prison authorities. They were even allowed to give an exhibition for the public to attend. Most of the artists made little figures or statues out of a combination of bread and plaster of Paris. These were attractive and would fetch a fair price.

Hepper was very well treated in prison, although like most prisoners he complained of the food. He was allowed to paint, and produced several pictures from memory. He painted a bull-fight and had evidently been a close student of the art of bull-fighting. Another picture he painted was of Lake Como in Italy, showing a large house where Mussolini used to stay. His ideas were not always so peaceful. He had a very realistic dream of London after an atomic bomb attack, with Trafalgar Square, for some reason, being flooded after all the buildings had been hit. He wanted permission to do three murals of London, New York and Moscow, as he visualised them after atomic attacks. 'In my dream', he said, 'it looked strange and beautiful.' The Governor can hardly have agreed, for he refused permission.

About his own case he talked incessantly. He seemed to be trying to remember what had happened in February. He had had a bad accident in 1947, and this, coupled with his asthma, made him a chronic invalid. In prison he would sometimes wear a sort of handkerchief round his head and complain of bad headaches. In Brighton he gave a pavement exhibition of his pictures and would make as much as £150 per month by selling them. Often his headaches would make him feel ill. One day he left his stand and sat in a shelter in

an armchair trying to relieve his feelings by the use of what
he called an 'atomiser'. A tall, thin man of good education
called B., aged about fifty, came up and sitting down next to
Hepper opened up a conversation with him. B. said that he
had long suffered from asthma as well, and would let Hepper
have some drugs to relieve the pain, as he greatly admired
Hepper's pictures. Those drugs were chocolate containing
opium, and Hepper paid ten shillings per half-dozen. Hepper
said that he saw B. about three times every week on the
front at Brighton. He liked B. and thought that B. let him
have the drugs out of kindness and not in order to make
money. He (Hepper) had therefore decided not to give the
police a correct description of the man. Hepper had been
taking opium in ever increasing quantities during the three
months preceding what he described as his 'black-out', in
February. He believed that B. was still in Brighton, walking
regularly on the promenade and peddling drugs, which he
obtains by post from some middleman in Liverpool. Hepper
admitted that this opium addiction had a great effect on
him. The dreams and the relief from pain were wonderful.
But B. bears an overwhelming share of the blame for whatever Hepper did. The law should have no mercy on drug-
peddlars.

Hepper seemed genuinely puzzled about what had
happened in connection with his crime. He thought and
spoke and even wrote about it a great deal. He used to say,
'I am convinced I did not do it', or 'I am convinced that I
could not have done it' (giving a physical reason). He was
almost equally convinced that someone else, whom he named,
had done it. Unlike most other prisoners, including murderers, he showed signs of being very worried, although his
face would light up when I got him to talk of his interests in
art or politics. He would stand for minutes looking at a shrub.
He even started to take an interest in religion. One day he
went up to a prisoner and asked, 'Do you obtain any solace
from religion?' The prisoner answered, 'I never took an
interest when things were going all right for me, and I am
not going to start now.' Hepper, although not an orthodox
Christian, believed in a personal God and in survival after

death. 'I believe we are often inhabited by a Spirit. When
we die the Spirit departs from the body.'

I asked him what had been the happiest time in his life.
He replied that he had never been happy except perhaps in
his childhood. He had, for an artist, an unusual aversion to
women. 'A woman is like a snake. It has a beautiful glossy
skin, but it is very vicious and very dangerous.'

The prison officers even allowed him to pick a daisy or a
dandelion as he walked slowly around the uneven circle in
the exercise yard. He was willing to talk to anyone and made
quite a friend of an intelligent young man who was being
sent to Broadmoor for a completely motiveless crime and of
a young artist who had, for no apparent reason, burned down
a Dutch barn. Hepper was always attentive and courteous
to everybody. He presented pictures to the Chief Prison
Doctor and to the Governor. On the whole he was well-liked
in the prison. The rule that good prison officers observe is to
ignore entirely the crimes alleged against a man and treat
him on his merits and behaviour in prison. No fault could be
found with Hepper judged by this test.

In politics he described himself as a Socialist. He was
strongly opposed to capitalism as well as Fascism, and held
an apparently genuine belief that the Americans are war-
mongers. 'We Chelsea artists', he would say, 'do not fall for
this barbarian propaganda.' Yet he had worked for the
Americans for years, and found them good employers,
although he complained that they made little use of his
secret reports. They had given him excellent references when
later he secured a job with the B.B.C. as a translator.

Hepper with his courtly manner and melancholy smile
remains an enigma. I doubt whether anyone will ever know
what really went on in the mind of the man who looked so
gentle.

Wells was an entirely different type of murderer. He had
killed a waitress with whom he had been living. 'I have not the
slightest recollection of anything that happened that night',
he said to me. He had been drinking very heavily for years
and on this occasion had evidently killed a girl of whom he
was very fond, in a senseless drunken fury. Wells was about

fifty-five years of age and was an outstandingly cheerful prisoner who used to walk about with a chequered handkerchief hanging out of his pocket and the air of an amiable buccaneer. He expected and wished to be hanged. 'I am a firm believer in capital punishment', he said to me once. 'For my own sake I would rather get it over with now than linger for years in captivity and emerge an old and broken man. I have had a good life and, apart from this terrible thing, I have no regrets.' At his trial an effort was made by his counsel to save him from the gallows—but he gave little or no assistance and in due course his real wish was fulfilled.

By contrast to these two murderers awaiting trial, I met later a murderer who had been reprieved and had served eight years of his sentence already. He was a young Yorkshireman with red hair who had murdered his wife, when very young. His face was deathly pale and nearly always expressionless. He had been transferred to Maidstone for special training—presumably because the Home Office intended that he should be released before long. This murderer sat next to me at table for nearly two months and I became convinced of the fact that few men could serve so long a sentence in the confined conditions of British gaols without having their faculties seriously impaired.

A prisoner I met in Brixton awaiting trial was D. He was trying to get himself certified 'unfit to plead'. He expected a sentence of fourteen years, if convicted, but if the doctors decided that he was insane he would be transferred to a civilian mental hospital, such as Crowthorne, where he hoped to stage his 'recovery' within a year or so. In any event it would be easy to escape from Crowthorne, he said, and if he could remain free for fourteen days he could not be arrested or detained without being certified all over again. D. was very thorough in his plans but he nearly made a literally fatal error. In his efforts to simulate insanity, he decided to *appear* to try to commit suicide. He made his bedsheet into a sort of rope, tied it to the window bars and rolled off the bed so that the sheet would strangle him. He timed this performance for a few minutes before the prison officers would normally enter his cell. Unfortunately for him

the routine was changed on this particular morning. The
officers opened the cells on the other side of the block first
and some thirty minutes elapsed before they reached D.'s
cell. It was touch and go for some hours, but D. survived.
Oddly enough he did not feel much pain when he strangled
himself and lost consciousness very rapidly. But the after-
effects were exceedingly painful. The next time he tried the
same trick he was very careful to arrange for a fellow-
prisoner to find him quickly. (He staged this attempted
suicide in the lavatory, using the lavatory chain.) His
fellow-prisoner even agreed to let D. appear to give him a
belting and add verisimilitude to the whole affair. It is quite
extraordinary to what lengths some prisoners will go to help
their 'mates' without any apparent hope of reward.

D. looked very like George Raft and was clean and careful
about his personal appearance. He had certainly succeeded
in 'foxing' some of the prison officers whose duty it is to
report on all suspected mental cases. His normal method of
evading prison sentences throughout the world had been to
get himself deported. He had had three or four different
passports, but being a British subject he had no hope of
being deported from this country and had to try the more
difficult method of simulating insanity. He was forty-one
years old and had left his father (who was high up in the
prison service in Australia) at the age of thirteen and run
away to sea to start the strange Odyssey of his life. I asked
him how he had found British prisons. 'Diabolical', was all
he would say. Yet he had to admit that the prison officers, or
'screws' as they are called in the vernacular, treated everyone
fairly and well. 'Most people inside try to help one another.
If only', he sighed, 'they could be the same outside.' In spite
of all his toughness and his deliberate dedication of his life
to crime and violence, this man possessed good qualities. One
was reminded of Robert Louis Stevenson: 'All his life long
the desire of good is at his heels, the implacable hunter.'

Perhaps the best friend I had in prison was R., a Pole,
who escaped a murder charge only by (perhaps literally) a
hair's breadth. He had hit his wife's lover on the head with
a hammer, and was serving a sentence of three years for

unlawful wounding and grevious bodily harm. But ethically this man was not to blame by the standards of his own country. A Pole who is dishonoured in this way feels it is his duty to go to any lengths to vindicate his honour. In this case the circumstances were particularly tragic. R. came from Lvov, and had been a fighter-pilot when war broke out. Inevitably he was shot down after a fortnight, but he managed to get to France where he joined the French Air Force. He came to Britain in 1940 and served with the R.A.F. throughout the war. When the war ended, he settled down in the West Country and married a pretty girl. There were children born of the marriage—of whom he was very proud. One day he opened a drawer in the bedroom and, finding his wife's diary in it, glanced at it out of curiosity. To his astonishment it contained details of her delight at the regular rendezvous she held with a named man who was a close friend of theirs and a fellow employee. He warned his wife that the affair must come to an end and secured the man's promise that he would not see her again. But later on the affair continued. He went to his employers and asked them, whatever happened, to see that the other man and he would never meet in the course of business. This proved impossible —and the obvious result occurred. R. armed with a hammer attacked his wife's paramour who had only a chisel with which to defend himself. R. himself was hurt, but it seems a miracle that the man he attacked was not killed. I asked R., 'How do you manage to hit a man on the head with a hammer hard enough to hurt him badly but not kill him?' He answered, 'I do not know, but that is exactly what I intended and what happened. Most Poles would have killed him and have intended to kill him.'

One of the most pathetic aspects of this case was that Lvov was officially ceded to the Soviet Union by wartime agreement between Stalin, Roosevelt and Churchill. It does not even enjoy the dubious advantage of Polish Communist rule as against direct rule by the Soviet Union. R. is a Polish patriot who would never dream of changing his nationality. He knows that he can never return to his native land. It was strange that the British Government should fête the men who held his country in subjection, Bulganin and Krushchev, while he wore a suit of prison grey for maintaining the standards of honour which prevailed in his country before we betrayed it. The attitude of his wife was creditable. She was desperately sorry for what she had done and was waiting eagerly for the day he would come out of prison.

R. was the only welder in the prison. The prison officers concerned with urgent repairs liked to work on Saturday afternoons so that they could work overtime, but they could not work without R. (universally known as 'Popski'). As they never even gave him a packet of cigarettes, he went 'on strike' one Saturday and, despite many threats, they could do nothing about it. If R. made up his mind about some-thing he was more obstinate than any mule. On this occasion he was more than justified—and he won his battle.

One of the best-liked prisoners was 'Willie', an excellent organist of about fifty years of age. He had a face which somehow combined intelligence with extreme simplicity. He was an obvious idiot and yet he was talented and kindly, and gifted with the most genuine ability to laugh at his own gaffes. He could have been persuaded to do anything. Some monstrous young man had imposed on him, extracted his money from him, blackmailed him and finally—on his own 'tip'—been found in bed with him. 'Willie' had pleaded guilty to the charge of indecency and been stupid enough to be defended by counsel. As a result the judge had never had the opportunity of hearing 'Willie' talk, or he would have realised the truth—that anyone could persuade 'Willie' to do anything. I used to tell him that when we were both released I would persuade him to sleep with the lions at the Zoo, just to see whether the judge would be stupid enough to imagine evil in such a circumstance. I am sure that I could persuade 'Willie' to do something of this sort and that he could then be persuaded to plead guilty. Lord Goddard was on one occasion undoubtedly right when he said that it was not always to the advantage of a prisoner to be defended by counsel.

One of the nicest prisoners at Maidstone was a baronet and an Old Etonian, Sir G. M. He really had a very fine

record, having been a car designer, a pilot in the Royal
Flying Corps and a very well-known racing driver, who for
some years held the track record at Brooklands. He had
photographs in his cell of his plane in the Royal Flying Corps
in World War I. He was a tall fresh-complexioned gentleman
of just the same type as is to be seen in dozens in London
clubs in the West End. When I first met him, I called him
'Sir George' in conversation, rather as one would in making
the acquaintance of any knight or baronet in the outside
world. He told me, however, that he would prefer me to call
him 'George' as he did not want to invite the ridicule of the
other prisoners. He certainly did not invite ridicule at all
and was treated with considerable respect, even by the
Teddy-boys. He was the Roman Catholic Chapel leader and,
as such, had custody of the communion wine—a precious
commodity in prison.

His trouble was purely financial—obtaining credit without
disclosing that he was an undischarged bankrupt. It really
was tragic to see this man, with such a fine record, serving a
prison sentence for what, at the very worst, could be only
described as petty fraud. The sad sequel is that he took his
children, soon after his release, to stay at an hotel on the
south-west coast and was soon back in prison again for
running up credit at this hotel for less than £50. One story
he told me, which I feel sure is true, is that in World War I,
flying against the famous Richtoven Squadron, he was badly
shot up one day and was limping back to base when he saw
Richtoven himself. Richtoven pointed a finger towards his
base as if to say, 'I am going to let you get home—I am not
shooting a sitting bird.' Many years afterwards Sir George
met Richtoven and reminded him of the incident. Tragedies
like this remind one a little of the many A. E. Housman
poems.

> 'Shot? so quick, so clean an ending,
> Oh that was right lad, that was brave.
> Yours was not an ill for mending,
> 'Twas best to take it to the grave.'

If only Sir George had died a little earlier, he would have
been a hero with nothing to dim the lustre of his glory.

I feel that there is really a kink in men like this and that they cannot help what they do. Deliberate dishonesty seemed quite alien to his real character.

By contrast to Sir G. M. there was L., described by John Vidler, the Governor of Maidstone, as the worst man but one that he had ever seen in prison. He was a swarthy middle-aged Jew—a dealer in antiques. His crime was an attempted fraud on an insurance company. He was very active in obtaining for himself contraband food of different kinds and I was reliably informed that he paid £10 a week to an officer to smuggle tobacco in to him, which he could exchange for the contraband food. He was very nearly caught on several occasions and on two occasions his accomplice was caught and was sent back to Wandsworth. Soon after I arrived, he came up to me and said that he would like to give me a quarter-ounce of tobacco 'because I like you'—pause— 'and because you might be able to get me half a pint of milk from the kitchen'. This was quite typical of his general behaviour.

The following afternoon he told me at great length and with great pride a long story about how he had cheated a widower of many thousands of pounds. This widower he discovered to be a wealthy man and to be devoted to the memory of his wife. L. managed to get himself invited to lunch as an art connoisseur and caught sight of a photograph of the wife and said, 'What a magnificent subject for a picture she would be.' He spent two or three hours with the old man and said that the tears came quite genuinely to his eyes in talking about this dead lady. He represented himself to be the agent of Sir William Orpen, and finally obtained £18,000 for a picture by Sir William Orpen based on the photograph. Presumably Orpen might have got £2,000 or £3,000 at the most out of the £18,000. L. thought it a master stroke that he had sent in his bill for 250 guineas on top for giving his advice. He also said that the widower had been most impressed by his hiring two flunkeys to deliver the picture.

L. was undoubtedly one of those prisoners who corrupt young men by putting dishonest ideas into their heads.

I have described a few of the interesting characters whom I met in prison. But of course, the majority of prisoners are not interesting. A considerable proportion of them have obviously been handicapped by natural defects of intelligence or character. Many prisoners—the bulk of the recidivists—seem constitutionally incapable of getting away from crime. The man, for instance, who had the best job in Maidstone Prison was serving a sentence of corrective training. When he got out he was found a good job and everything was going well for him. He had been given every assistance by the prison authorities, particularly as his next sentence might well be preventive detention for seven or more years. Yet before long he made another 'mistake'—which was successfully hushed up. A month afterwards he stole a car and was back in prison again. Such cases as this are incomprehensible. There is no 'cure', although often after some twenty or thirty years they abandon their criminal habits. 'Maturation' is the word used to describe the process which exhausts their propensity to crime, but the reasons for maturation are not known.

The best description of prisoners is to be found in Dostoievsky's *House of the Dead*. He described the same unpredictable nature and unexpected loyalties as I found in English prisons in a slightly different form a hundred years later. Above all he captured the atmosphere of prison, although of course there was much more freedom as well as more cruelty and venality in Siberia under the Czars than in England in the middle of 'the century of the common man'.

CHAPTER XV

Prison Reform

PRISONS are establishments for the housing of prisoners.
The subject of prison reform should, therefore, start with
an examination of the average prison population. The object
of prison reform should be to make prisoners useful citizens
inside prison so that when they emerge from it they are
likely to continue to lead a useful life. The object of the
present prison system appears to be to confine prisoners in a
small space and in conditions where they are least likely to
be able to cause trouble or to escape—with the inevitable
consequence that the prisons are a financial burden on the
community.

It goes without saying that prisons should not be places
to which men want to go. Sentimentality on the subject of
prisons and prisoners is odious. Indeed, self-pity is the occu-
pational disease of prisoners and is accentuated by the fact
that the average prisoner can do little or nothing to help
himself while he is in prison. Any proposals which I make are
not designed to make the life of a prisoner easy and comfortable. They are designed to see that, while prison sentences
remain deterrent in effect, they do not corrupt or weaken the
characters of those who undergo them—as largely happens at
present. Talk about rehabilitation of prisoners is almost
entirely nonsense. Men are shut up for years doing false or
futile work, compelled to associate with real crooks and
perverts of all sorts, and then discharged with unstamped
cards and a couple of pounds in their pockets. It is beyond
my imagination how the Prison Commissioners, who are
responsible for this, can make themselves so ludicrous as to
talk about the regenerative and rehabilitative aspects of
prison life. Few men can come out of prison better than they

went in. The great majority come out far worse, weakened in mind and character.

The statistics about prisoners are extraordinarily interesting. For instance, of all prisoners convicted for the first time of serious offences, only about 25 per cent or less return. In the United States the corresponding figure is more like 50 per cent. In other words, twice as many American first offenders go back to prison as British first offenders. American prisons vary enormously from the most antiquated to the most modern types. In general, there is more freedom inside American prisons, because arms are used to guard them, but otherwise conditions in the older American prisons resemble conditions in our prisons. Violence is more usually employed by those in authority in the police and prison services in America than here. By and large, therefore, it cannot be claimed that life in British prisons is substantially more unpleasant than life in American prisons. The real explanation for the huge disparity between the proportions of American and British 'repeaters' must be elsewhere.

It is surely remarkable that about three out of four persons convicted for the first time of serious finger-printable offences and sentenced to from six months to five years should never return to prison. I have asked a large number of people, before informing them of the answer, what proportion they would expect not to return. The usual answer is that they would expect half. Their guess would be reasonably accurate for America and inaccurate here by a factor of 100 per cent. The man who would defend the present prison system would claim that its deterrent effect is responsible for the very large proportion of men who do not come back to prison after their first sentence. As against this view, there is the fact that improvements in conditions in prison have not produced any decrease in the proportion of the 'saved', but rather the reverse.

There are other statistics which appear to me highly relevant, if considered in conjunction with the rough figure of the three out of four first offenders who do not return. These are the figures showing the daily average populations of prisons and Borstals from 1890 to the present day. They are approximately as follows:

In 1890 there were approximately 18,000.

Rising between 1890 and 1904 to approximately 21,000.

Falling between 1910 and 1915 to approximately 10,000.

Between 1915 and 1940 fluctuating between approximately 10,000 and 13,000.

From 1945 to 1956 rising from 12,000 to approximately 23,000.

There was, therefore, no substantial increase after World War I—despite unemployment and the bitter disillusionment following the promise of 'a land fit for heroes to live in'. But after World War II there was a huge increase until today the prison population is more than twice what it was between the two wars and higher than it has been for seventy-five years—all this in spite of the low figure of unemployment, the Health Service and the rest of the apparatus of the Welfare State.

One last figure tells the tale. In each of the years 1926, 1927, 1928, 1929 and 1930, there were roughly the same number of convictions for serious offences as in 1952 or 1953. Yet the average prison population was double. There can be only one possible explanation of this. The judges of today award twice as severe sentences as the judges of a generation ago. This has been confirmed to me by the personal experience of a senior retired official who worked in the Court of Criminal Appeal from its inception in 1907. But it can easily be deduced from an analysis of the figures.

It is not my purpose in this chapter to comment on the changed attitude of the judges or to argue that there is probably a disturbingly substantial number of innocent men in prison. I am here writing about prison reforms and have quoted these statistics to show that the views taken by the judges concerning the conduct of first offenders today are twice as harsh as those taken by the great judges of twenty-five years ago. This must involve the proposition that there are many persons in prison who would not have been sent there at all by the contemporaries of Lord Atkin and Lord Justice Scrutton and that there are also many prisoners whose sentences are much longer than they would have been a generation ago.

Moreover, if three out of four first offenders never come back to prison, it must be the case that over half the prison population are not real criminals but have been involved in one incident or series of incidents at a particular phase of their lives as a result of which they have 'got into trouble'. John Vidler said to me one day, 'Ninety per cent of prisoners could be let out on parole to work as free men during the day and would return in the evening.' He almost certainly put the percentage too high. In any event I should not advocate that such methods should be used for any large percentage of the prison population. They are proving highly successful for men serving the last twelve months of very long sentences and undoubtedly ease the transition from prison to normal life.

What is needed is an entirely new administration of the prisons with an entirely new directive. The directive should be on the following lines: 'The policy of the Government is that within a period of three years the entire prison system should be reorganised so that the vast majority of prisoners are doing useful work. The prisons will become self-supporting and the prisoners be enabled to save a sufficient sum of money to give them a fair start in life at the end of their sentences. In this process, there will be a proper system of segregation by which dangerous prisoners of all kinds are kept together in confinement and not allowed to mix with other prisoners; homosexuals who try to corrupt other prisoners will be assigned to a special camp of their own; first offenders will be kept together and other offenders assigned to camps or prisons which are suitable to their known character. The majority of prisoners will work on the land either in areas requisitioned by the Government on prison farms, or on private farms being hired out to the farmers. A considerable programme of camp-building will be immediately undertaken to enable this dispersal of prisoners to take place. Existing prisons will be rearranged for the much smaller prison population to have more freedom inside the prison walls and above all to enable them to do really

useful work. The co-operation of the trade unions is being
enlisted in order to see that the type of work so done need
not be stupid and degrading but can approximate to that
done in many types of civilian employment. Prison officers
must regard themselves as men who must get the maximum
work out of the prisoners in their charge, wherever possible,
by being friendly and co-operative.'

To those unacquainted with the facts, it may appear that
this plan would leave the doors wide open to a large number
of escapes. In fact the number of escapes from open camps is
quite small. Of the two hundred or more prisoners who are
given seven days' leave every year, about three months
before their release, all return on the appointed day—one or
two perhaps a little late. For ordinary prisoners escape offers
few attractions. Few of them have any money. Of the small
fraction who have, only a minute number possess enough to
be able to plan an escape from the country. If they did
escape, they would not get far. The modern State is too full of
official requirements of one kind or another for a man
to be able to conceal his identity for long without great
difficulty.

In any event, no great harm is done if a prisoner does
escape. It is highly probable that he will find himself in a
police court again very soon—and be recognised. It is almost
certain that he will be caught eventually, and in any case
he would have to have been released at the end of his
sentence. He is not a dangerous animal likely to wound or to
kill but a pathetic figure on the run. (I am, of course, here
excluding the class of violent criminals, who should be kept
in close confinement.) It would be monstrous to veto a
plan which could save the country a large sum of money
every year as well as improve so greatly the conduct of the
State towards prisoners, on the ground that it might involve
the escape for short periods of a small number of prisoners.
Moreover, the danger of any large increase could be met by
requiring prisoners to accept as a condition of their obtaining
the advantages of the new system, that they would undergo
heavier punishment than is now given for escapes and
attempted escapes.

The punishment for escapes is already severe in most cases. Escapees, in addition to losing remission, are sent to prisons where they are not only kept in strict confinement but made to wear patches and parade separately from their fellow-prisoners. The light is kept on in their cells at night and most of their clothes are taken from them. They lead an unpleasant existence. One man escaped from camp while I was at Maidstone. He had only five months to go. Within that period he was back in Maidstone awaiting transfer to Wandsworth, with a total sentence of about five years, made up of misdemeanours committed while 'on the run'. His reappearance was no encouragement to any other prisoner to follow his example. Prison officers are not greatly concerned when prisoners on 'outside parties' or in camps escape. They sometimes even tell them where the nearest railway station is. They know that the men will be caught quickly enough and that it is unnecessary to treat their temporary absence as a major tragedy. The escape of dangerous or violent prisoners would be an entirely different matter.

The implementation of this plan could not be effectively carried out by the present Prison Commissioners. The present Director of Prison Administration is a Quaker and former Borstal Governor. When he came to Maidstone, he spent most of his time on the kind of inspection which a Quartermaster performs as a matter of routine in the Army. He is the last person one would dream of employing for the positive task of reorganising prison administration. Here a business man is required with experience in building and organising 'shadow' factories in a hurry. He should be assisted by one or two farmers with first-class records for reclaiming derelict land and by suitable advisers in other kinds of industry. These men could enlist the support of Governors in removing the atmosphere of stagnation and decay which clings to every British prison, including Maidstone.

In one respect, prison administration seems to be even more restrictive than it was sixty years ago. Both *Reading Gaol* and *De Profundis* were written by Oscar Wilde in prison —the latter in the form of a long letter to a friend. Today

prisoners are not allowed to have paper to write on—except
for the issue of a four-page letter every fortnight. They may
apply for an exercise book and obtain permission to have
one, but if they do it is subject to the following rules which
appear on the cover of the book:

'1.   This notebook is granted for the study of ——————
and is to be used for this purpose only.

2.   If Rule 1 is broken, or if any pages are removed, the
book will be withdrawn.

3.   Entries in foreign languages must be limited to educational notes necessary for a continued study on the subject.

4.   You may, if you wish, take this book out with you when
you are discharged, providing that you have not

(i) written in it about any of the following matters:
Your own life.
The lives of other prisoners or ex-prisoners.
Your own offences or sentences, or those of other
prisoners or ex-prisoners.
Prison conditions.
Methods of committing crime.

(ii) drawn or painted anything depicting prisoners,
members of the prison staff, prison conditions or
matters related to crime.

(iii) written in it any notes in shorthand or cypher.

5.   If you wish to take this book out with you on discharge
you should submit it to the Governor, with an application
for retention, 28 days before you are due to be discharged.'

There was a recent case where a prison officer became
involved in serious trouble originating from the fact that he
had been willing to smuggle short stories written by a
prisoner out of prison. Surely prisoners should be allowed to
write and sell imaginative work unconnected with prison or
crime and to have half the proceeds credited to them, and
half given to some prison fund. This happens in Spain where
prisoners are allowed to sell their works of art.

In the process of effecting a material change in the conditions of prison life for the majority of prisoners, a great change
could and should be made in the relationship between the
prison officers and the men. Many Prison Governors and

Deputy Governors have themselves given an abominable example to their staff by saying to prisoners after accepting or rejecting their applications, 'Get out'. This has been a common practice in the prison service to the knowledge of everyone from the Chairman of the Commissioners downwards. What conceivable justification there has been for it is hard to say. It is as if the senior officers of the prison service concerned were trying to impress on the prisoners that bad manners extended everywhere behind prison bars.

Governors should insist on reasonable courtesy being shown by both officers and men and should set an example themselves. There must be some extraordinary regulation on this subject. When I left Maidstone, I had a long friendly conversation with the present Governor about prisons. As I left the room he said, 'Do you mind shaking hands with me now? I shall see you in the morning in the office, of course, but that is a different matter.' When I saw him the following morning, he adopted the same procedure with me as with other prisoners—as was perfectly right. But one wonders why a Governor should not shake hands with prisoners in his office on the last occasion that he sees them.

I am not suggesting that there should be familiarity between officers and men or that prison discipline should not be maintained. In good units of the Army there is a tradition of 'on parade, on parade; off parade, off parade', which enables a relationship of mutual respect to be developed. With some necessary modifications a similar tradition could be introduced in the prison service. I see no reason why it should not be adopted as a normal practice that officers should say 'Good morning' to the men when they open their cells in the morning. One officer did this at Maidstone, and although he found that many prisoners could hardly believe their ears, he told me that as a policy it paid good dividends.

One particular form of familiarity between officers and men is outrageous. There are a number of obvious homosexuals in all prisons. They are called by other prisoners by feminine Christian names, such as 'Dorothy' and 'Jenny'. This in itself should not be countenanced

by the prison officers, but it is really disgraceful that
the officers themselves should adopt the same habit.
I have even heard them say, 'Jennie, you naughty girl,
hurry up or you will be late.' There should be a very strict
rule that the flaunting of homosexuality in any form is not
to be tolerated.

This is a serious matter as many homosexuals, like drug
addicts, seek to entice others to imitate them. I saw them
succeed twice at Maidstone with young men who would
never have felt the inclination in normal circumstances.
It is not an easy subject to analyse, as some prisoners who are
homosexuals are in prison for different offences from homosexuality. There was for instance a man whom I knew very
well, whose offence was 'marrying' in church an American
sergeant. It was a white wedding. He said to me, I believe
sincerely, 'Eric and I swore eternal love and we thought it a
great idea that our love should be blessed just as the love of
normal people is blessed.' There must have been an
element of truth in this, as otherwise 'Eric' and he could
have adopted a far less dangerous means of obtaining the
appearance of legal matrimony.

John Vidler believed that it would be utterly wrong to
segregate homosexuals. Many of them, he said, could only
be cured by mixing with normal people. But there should
surely be this safeguard introduced for the sake of the impressionable young men in prison—that any homosexual who
persists in flaunting his homosexuality or corrupts another
prisoner should be sent to a special prison where he can
only hope to corrupt men of the same kind as himself.

I know that my views on this subject have already intensely annoyed some well-known people, but I adhere to
them from personal knowledge. The facts are too unpleasant
for including in a book. In all this, however, I am not
expressing any opinion as to whether it is right for society to
send to prison adults indulging in homosexuality, if they do
not corrupt young persons or other men. Formally to
legitimise buggery would appear to be a somewhat excessive
step. But I do not believe that any prosecution should take
place where no corruption of innocent persons or young

people has been proved. Moreover, it seems needless cruelty that some of the prisoners incarcerated for these offences should have to serve such long sentences in such unpleasant conditions. There is a strong case to be made in favour of many of the homosexuals in prison—but it has been over-stated and overlooks the proselytising element in so many of them.

Here then, in conclusion, are the proposals I would make for the reform of the prison service:

(1) *Work*

Prisoners should be engaged on useful productive work instead of on futile or false work. There is no reason whatever why well over half the prisoners now in prisons should not be engaged on the land. The Government should requisition areas of derelict land, reclaim it and run the farms efficiently with prison labour. As a result of so doing, the prison service could very quickly cease to be a burden on the Exchequer and could pay its way. It would have the added advantage of raising the status of the job of a prison officer, who would then become, not a man employed to prevent the escape of an undesirable person, but a man engaged on useful work for the benefit of the country. His pay could also probably be increased in the process.

(2) *Saving*

As a result of this, it should be possible to pay prisoners a reasonable sum of money, say half of what they would get in the outside world for their services and they should be taught to save. THE TWO THINGS WHICH CAN REDEEM A MAN ARE TO TEACH HIM TO WORK AND TO SAVE. UNDER THE PRESENT SYSTEM, THE PRISONER CAN BE TAUGHT NEITHER.

(3) *Segregation of Prisoners*

It is most important that prisoners convicted of particularly repulsive crimes and likely to corrupt young prisoners, should be segregated from those young prisoners. In particular, brothel-keepers, and people in for similar offences, should not be mixed up with young thieves, etc. One prisoner like Joseph Grech can do more harm in one day to the minds of a dozen prisoners than could be put right by a whole bench of Bishops on an eternity of Sundays.

(4)   *Church Services*

The Archbishop of Canterbury should see that there are first-class clergymen available in all prisons and particularly in local prisons, such as Wormwood Scrubs. (I like the Reverend Davies very much but he cannot possibly do half his work.) There cannot be a better audience imaginable for preachers than the prison population. It is disgraceful that the Archbishop and the Bishops ignore this crying need.

(5)   *Homosexuals*

A great deal of harm is done (*a*) by homosexuals directly corrupting young boys who would not otherwise have those tendencies, (*b*) by friction between the 'queers' as they are called and the ordinary thieves, etc., (*c*) by the open toleration of homosexuality practised by officers. Homosexuals who flaunt their perversion should be segregated from other prisoners. Any prison officer calling a homosexual by a feminine Christian name should be disciplined.

(6)   *The Administration of the Prison Service*, which is deplorably inefficient, should be taken over by some practical person from outside it. As an illustration, it takes about three months to answer a petition. A thorough overhaul from the point of view of business efficiency is needed of the whole system.

(7)   *Manners*

Every official of the prison service from Commissioners downwards should be directed that it is their duty at all times to be well-mannered in their behaviour towards prisoners and to expect that the prisoners are equally well-mannered in their behaviour in return. In future any Governor who says 'Get out' to a prisoner coming before him on an application should be summarily dismissed from the service. The only way to teach manners to other people is to practise them yourself.

(8)   *Exercise*

The requirement that prisoners should get one hour's exercise should be strictly enforced and it should be real exercise. Time should not be deducted for waiting on parade while being counted, etc. This will mean that prisoners will get an extra twenty minutes exercise as at present they really only get about forty minutes exercise a day.

(9) *Sanitation*

The sanitary arrangements should be improved. This, however, is a point so much stressed by everybody that I do not consider it needs any further comment from me.

(10) *Incentives*

The whole of the outside world that is sensible works on incentives. It would be to the advantage of the prisoners and the prison staff and ultimately the public that the whole prison system should be geared to a system of incentives. It should be a clearly accepted principle throughout the prison service in relation to work that so far as possible it should be organised on the following principles:

(*a*) that the officers supervising the work receive a proportion of money for the extra work done.

(*b*) that the prisoners involved in the work receive another proportion of money for the work done.

(*c*) that the inter-relation of the above-named proportions is known to both sides so that they both have a common interest which may transcend the normal barrier between officer and prisoner.

(11) *Stamps*

The cards of a prisoner should be stamped for the period during which he has been in prison, so that he does not face the dilemma on release of whether or not to disclose to a potential employer his prison record. The cost of the stamps from the Post Office would merely transfer money from one Government department to another and would impose no added burden on the Exchequer.

(12) *Informers*

Except in the case of very serious charges, no use should be made of anonymous informers.

CHAPTER XVI

Coming Out

WHEN Dostoievsky came out of prison he wrote, 'O insupportable joy!' He had spent five years in Siberia roughly one hundred years ago, and witnessed terrible floggings. He had been in prison hospital with men in the process of being flogged to death. He had been able to pay for an unofficial servant, who had cooked him a steak, or some other meat dish, every day. The day of his release was a day of enormous happiness.

Most prisoners seem to feel very different. This is not to say that they are not glad that their sentence has been served, but that they fear the return to normal life. The main reason for this is financial. But there are other reasons as well. In prison everything is done for a man. He is called in the morning, issued with his breakfast, dinner and tea, marched to and from work and is in effect put to bed early in the evening. It is all very much as if he were back in a rather grim kind of school. Somebody is there to look after him all the time. In consequence, when most prisoners go out of the gates feeling lonely and unaided, there must be a sense of helplessness in face of the unexpected noise and bustle of the world. For quite a while even I found it distinctly unpleasant to walk from Sloane Avenue to Sloane Square.

But far more serious is the hunger. When I came out of prison, I looked lean and fit. Two months later people said to me, 'My word, you *have* put on weight!' They were quite right. But I had to put on weight. That lean fit look which a man has when he leaves prison is most deceptive. Although I lived and ate well after my release, I was almost permanently hungry for more than two months. So were most other prisoners to whom I have talked, including men as tough as

Edward Chapman, the former safe-breaker who pretended
to turn spy for the Nazis and double-crossed them.

If this applied to a man like myself, who had not lacked the
means to buy the best food, or had the worry of not knowing
how to pay for his board and lodging, what must it be like
for prisoners who are discharged with a few shillings in their
pockets? It is not that the food in prison is insufficient.
There is enough bread to keep a normal man from hunger.
The authorities claim that they give a balanced diet. When
I was in prison I never complained about the food. But its
content is such that on release the ex-prisoner who can
afford to eat steaks and eggs in abundance, still feels hungry
from time to time during the day. The diet is enough for a
man living a half-existence, but when he returns to full life,
he must rebuild his strength.

*Yet the average prisoner goes out of the prison gates with enough
money to last him a couple of days at the most—and many are
released on Saturdays.*

Take, for instance, the case of a friend of mine in Maidstone Prison, who was manager for one of the most famous
firms of chartered accountants and did three years for
intercepting some of the fees due to his firm for the work he
had done. He wrote me that he had received three shillings,
'presumably a bob a year'. A common amount is ten
shillings. Two or three pounds is well above the average.
I met one man who underwent a religious conversion to the
Christian Scientists and received ten pounds on release—
as do all Christian Scientists on their first release from prison.
The Roman Catholic Church sometimes provides an extra
pound or two in special cases. I never heard of a case where
the Church of England gave any help. But the Church of
England 'padres' cannot personally be blamed as they are
disgracefully underpaid. Four years ago Prison Chaplains
drew £450 per annum—less than the average earnings of a
worker at Austins.

The great majority of prisoners have no money of their
own. If they had a few pounds when they were arrested, they
spent it on their defence in one way or another. At least 90
per cent of those released from Maidstone Prison while I

G

was there had nothing at all. Even more tragic was the
fact that many of them were without friends. One of the best
men I met was a former regular lieutenant-colonel with a
really first-class war record. He had been through the
campaign in the Desert right from the beginning and had
then gone to Burma. After the war his wife developed an
incurable illness. He retired and commuted his pension to
enable her to die in comfort with him at her side in Switzer-
land. After her death he had let everything go and eventually
'got into trouble'. Exactly what the trouble was I did not
know, although it was financial. Two nights before his
release, he said to me, 'Now the battle begins all over again',
with such an air of sadness that I was deeply shocked. He
really had not a single friend in the world. I arranged for a
friend of mine to meet him in a café near Piccadilly soon
after his release. His hands were trembling and he looked
utterly forlorn. Surely some effort should be made to help
men like this who have given the best years of their lives to
the service of their country. He was a very able man and had
even become a Bachelor of Law of London University in his
spare time. The lack of effort made to rehabilitate ex-
prisoners of this sort is wasteful as well as inhuman.

Of course, it is fatally easy for many of the younger men
to drift into a life of crime or to earn a precarious living by
means bordering on crime. Along comes a man who has his
eye on a youth just released from prison, and who gives him a
few pounds when he most desperately needs it. What with the
prospect of a little easy money and the feeling that he must
do something to repay his benefactor, the youth is wide
open to suggestions which can only lead him downhill.

Former prisoners who really try to get hard and honest
work have great difficulty over their cards. These have not
been stamped during their period in prison. A prospective
employer is, therefore, likely to want to know why. The ex-
prisoner is faced with an agonising alternative. Is he to tell
the truth—in which case he may lose his job? Or is he to
start off his new job by telling a lie?

The public constantly hears of claims from official sources
that great efforts are made to help in the rehabilitation of

ex-convicts. More than thirty-five years ago the then Home
Secretary granted remissions affecting 11,000 prisoners 'and
at a stroke struck five hundred years of imprisonment and
penal servitude from the prison population'. He said, 'I am
glad to be able to tell the House that no evil results of any
kind have followed from this.' He pleaded for 'a calm and
dispassionate recognition of the rights of the accused against
the State, and even of convicted criminals against the State,
a constant heart-searching by all charged with the duties of
punishment, a desire and eagerness to rehabilitate in the world
of industry all those who have paid their dues in the hard
coinage of punishment, tireless efforts towards the discovery
of curative and regenerating processes, and an unfaltering
faith that there is a treasure, if you can only find it, in the
heart of every man.' The name of this unpractical idealist?
Winston Churchill.

The regular prison population is now at its peak of about
twice the number that were in prison between the two wars
—in spite of the Welfare State. The main reason for this is
the one I gave in the preceding chapter—that judges are
very much more severe in their sentences than they were
before the war. Whether right or wrong, this is deliberate
policy designed to check crime by increasing the penalties
for crime. But it should also increase the obligation on society
to give a helping hand to those who have undergone the
increased sentences.

I have met prisoners who were with me at Maidstone and
were still looking for jobs two months after their release.
It is, of course, much more difficult for a black-coated worker
than for other kinds of workers. Of those prisoners who are
sentenced to corrective training, only a fraction in fact
receive training in a trade in which they can find a job on their
release. Much of the blame for this state of affairs, and for the
grotesquely low wages of about half a crown a week earned
by prisoners, is placed by the prison authorities on the trade
union movement. But no serious effort has been made to
enlist the sympathy of the trade unions. They could hardly
be expected to act on their own. I know that men like Tom
Williamson and Tom O'Brien of the T.U.C. and the late

Arthur Deakin would have the same approach to this problem
as had Churchill in the speech which I have quoted from
Hansard of 20th July, 1910. By agreement with the trade
unions the Home Secretary could put an end to the false
or futile work being done by 99 per cent of the prisoners.
They could do useful work to earn them enough money on
their release to look the world in the face. In Australia
prisoners get £20 on their release. They can then have no
excuse on financial grounds if they turn to crime immediately.
No man in this country should emerge from prison after
'doing a stretch' without £20.

In one respect the Prison Commissioners actually prevent
a prisoner from receiving help. There was a man in Maidstone with me who had a magnificent war record as a
parachutist. His offence was smuggling—on a large scale,
it is true. He is an Irishman. His conduct was exemplary
and he was made a 'leader' and caretaker of the Roman
Catholic chapel. I made arrangements for him to be
welcomed when he was due for 'leave'—seven days release
granted to prisoners who serve three or more years. I
notified the Governor and the Chaplain that I had made these
arrangements. I even told the New Bridge that I wanted to
help this prisoner and that I was experiencing difficulty. The
New Bridge declined to help, and my friend, in entire ignorance
of the arrangements I had made, declined the 'leave'. An
ex-prisoner is prevented by prison regulations from com-
municating with a prisoner. This may be a sound rule in
many cases, but in a case like this it is the height of insanity.
Often the only man who will really help a prisoner, is another
prisoner.

I can understand the attitude of someone who will say in
reply to all this, 'Before I start worrying about ex-convicts, I
will try to help the many people who are in desperate
trouble through no fault of their own.' Certainly there is no
need for sentimentality which does nothing but harm. The
ex-prisoner who seeks pity is contemptible. But most people
would agree with the youthful Winston Churchill that, 'The
mood and temper of the public in regard to the treatment
of crime and criminals is one of the most unfailing tests of

the civilisation of any country'. By that test this country today, if weighed in the balance, would be found wanting.

Oscar Wilde wrote in *De Profundis* that 'the working-class are much more understanding about people who have been to prison than the middle and upper classes. They speak of their neighbours as having been in trouble.' There is much truth in this. I received many letters from working people— not only from my old constituency—offering me what help they could on my release from prison. Owing to certain newspaper reports they believed that I was destitute. I received no similar messages from the vast majority of my friends in more exalted spheres, some of whom were under some kind of obligation to me. The saying of Jesus, that 'it is easier for a camel to go through the eye of a needle than for a rich man to enter the Kingdom of Heaven', was clearly an intentional exaggeration, but it remains fundamentally true today. We are constantly reminded of Lord Acton's dictum: 'All power corrupts. Absolute power corrupts absolutely.' This dictum appears to be true of wealth also. There are, of course, great and honourable exceptions. Moreover, charity is generally best given anonymously through institutions which are administered by people of common sense and good will. Yet it is amazing that the Discharged Prisoners Aid Society should be permanently operating on utterly inadequate funds, while animal charities of all kinds are glutted with gifts and bequests, and even in one case have a multi-millionaire for a treasurer.

A civilian who acted as Assistant Chaplain at Maidstone told me that over many years he had lent selected prisoners £10 on their release. In every case but one the money had been returned. He believed that the fact that there was a personal relationship of trust between himself and each prisoner made a great difference. A similar experience was had by a client of mine who had served with his solicitor a short sentence at Maidstone for the offence of 'showing favour'. On his release—and, as he told me, largely because of his admiration for John Vidler—he decided to notify the Labour Exchanges that he would employ ex-prisoners. When they were taken on by his firm, he made a point of telling them that he was an ex-prisoner himself. He found that the ex-prisoners proved just as honest and reliable as the remainder of his workers—and that there were some who were fanatically anxious to show their appreciation of his trust.

Other employers take a different view and they have every right to do so—unless they profess to be Christians. But whatever a man's opinions on religious or political matters he must be lacking in imagination if he does not appreciate the great satisfaction to be derived from investing in failure and proving right. It is easy to invest in success, but to find a man down and out with the added handicap of a prison sentence behind him and, having trusted him, to find one's trust repaid must be a fine experience. Stevenson was right about many prisoners and ex-prisoners when he wrote, 'A fool, a thief, the comrade of thieves, even here keeping the point of honour and the touch of pity, often repaying the world's scorn with service, often standing firm upon a scruple, and at a certain cost rejecting riches . . . everywhere the ensign of man's ineffectual goodness . . . they are condemned to some nobility; all their lives long, the desire of good is at their heels, the implacable hunter.'

Many a prisoner has come out of prison with 'the desire of good' and been unable to keep his good intentions. Of one thing I am certain. Our present prison system cannot have improved his character and is likely only to have done him harm. Much depends on the reception he gets in the world outside. If he had that best friend of all, a few pounds in his pocket, he would at least have a fair start in the ordeal of his return to a strange world. Not one prisoner in ten can 'see ahead' for so much as a week, when he leaves the prison gates.

CHAPTER XVII

Finding Out

AMAZING as it now seems to me, it was not until 1957 that I first came to realise that I might be an alcoholic. I had been made bankrupt. I had been divorced. I had been sent to prison for offences of which I was not guilty. All this had been largely due to my drinking habits. I had got into a number of 'scrapes' due to drink and been convicted three or four times of being drunk. Yet in spite of all this I did not regard myself as an alcoholic. I have never had delirium tremens. My drinking always appeared to me and to many other people to be controllable. The common definition of alcoholism is addiction to uncontrollable drinking. It is a most misleading definition. The test is not whether the drinking is controllable, but whether it is in fact controlled. Some acquaintances and at least two friends of mine were in many respects far worse than I and they did not regard themselves as alcoholics. So neither did I. (I now find it frightening to go into public houses where I know the habitués and ask myself how many of them are obvious alcoholics.)

In 1955, on coming out of prison, I met 'Sam' who was manager of a building business owned by a very close friend of mine, a hard-drinking Irishman. 'Sam' at the time was in the alcoholic ward of a hospital and came out on parole twice a week. His had been a very bad case of alcoholism. He had been in hospital before for months. The previous 'cure' had not been effective. Life had not been easy for him—to put it mildly—but since I met him he has not had a drink. He is, so far as one can tell, a remarkable example of an alcoholic who has conquered his weakness. It was 'Sam' who persuaded me in the summer of 1956 to see the doctor who had been largely responsible for his own deliverance. I went to see this doctor partly through a feeling of disgust with myself at my continued propensity to drink heavily, partly out of curiosity. The doctor did not try to persuade me that I was an alcoholic. He told me at the beginning of our conversation that his opinion on such a matter was of little importance; what mattered, he said, was my opinion and perhaps he could help by asking a few questions. Within an hour the questions which he asked with a melancholy, objective yet not unsympathetic manner, had convinced me that I must be an alcoholic.

First he asked me to tell him briefly about my life and particularly about the troubles I had had. He interrupted only when I had told him the bare facts about some evil which had befallen me. I had gone bankrupt. 'Do you think', he said, 'that drink had anything to do with your bankruptcy?' 'Of course it had', I replied. In every case, bankruptcy, divorce, prison and so on, I had to admit that drink had played an important part in my downfall. Then he asked, 'Why, knowing that drink had done you so much harm, did you go on drinking?' The question was unanswerable on any basis other than that I was suffering from some form of mental unbalance. I decided that this mental unbalance must be alcoholism, that anyone who, having got into trouble through drink twice, continues to drink must in practice be an alcoholic, and I went away that night convinced that I was one.

The doctor wished me to go into hospital, but I gave up drink then and there—for about three months. During the week after my decision to give up drink, I often swore to myself: 'I will kill myself rather than have another drink. This for me is a matter of life and death.' Over and over again I repeated to myself: 'I will kill myself rather than have another drink.' I believed that I had cured myself by self-hypnosis. Three months later, when a domestic trouble worried me again, I broke my oath. I went to Spain and there I broke it 'real good', as my American friends in Barcelona said. I had a wonderful time in Barcelona and in Madrid. Then for a while I lived alone in a chalet in

Alicante. I listened to the flamenca. One night when I had
had quite a lot to drink, I scribbled on a piece of paper:
>'This strange and lovely song
>>Older than sin,
>A lament for the fate of man,
>The despairing hope
>That one moment of beauty
>May prevail against the cold of eternity.

I was drinking heavily. I could feel the cold of eternity very
close to me. It did not frighten me, but it made me feel like
Elizabeth Barrett Browning must have felt—'I tell thee
hopeless grief is passionless . . .'.

One morning I decided that I must strike my tents and
be on the march again. So with some difficulty I came back
to England, determined this time to give up drink for ever.
I went into hospital and came out after a few days. For about
three months I was 'dry'. Then I broke out again, not badly
compared with past performances, but I knew how dangerous
it was. I have kept 'dry' for fairly long periods but always
slipped back. I have had what the alcoholic fraternity call
'skids'. With this record I know or, should I say, I hope I
know that for me to remain teetotal demands a fearful effort.
I can be cured of alcoholism only by curing myself of other
deep-rooted faults, of selfishness and of idleness. There is
another factor. Shakespeare, as always, had words for it
when he asked:

>'Canst thou not minister to a mind diseased,
>Pluck from the memory a rooted sorrow?'

'*Meliora cognosco, deteriora sequor.*' I see the madness, as did
James Thomson, and yet I have cheated myself, as he did.
He described the mental process superbly and exactly.
He wrote in *The City of Dreadful Night*:

>'They are most rational and yet insane,
>An outward madness not to be controlled,
>A perfect reason in the central brain
>That has no power but sitteth wan and cold
>And sees the madness and foresees as plainly
>The ruin in its path and trieth vainly
>To cheat itself, refusing to behold.'

I have been told that the manner of his death matched
these prophetic lines. Three days before he died Ford
Maddox Brown found him lying across a whelk-stall being
belaboured by the whelkman. He was drunk and destitute.
(The alcoholic, although broke, manages to get drunk.)
Brown took the poet back to his house and gave him a bed
and some decent clothes. The next day Robert Browning
came to tea. Thomson suddenly jumped up shouting, 'I am
a Bengal tiger!' and tried to attack Browning. Later he went
round to a third poet and clawed him grievously, shouting,
'I am a Bengal tiger!' He had a bad haemorrhage and was
taken to hospital to die. Thomson not only saw into the
mind of the alcoholic but described it with extraordinary
clarity and understanding. His genius was perfection at the
expense of life and he painted perfectly the shadow of his
own death.

But most alcoholics need not go the way that Thomson
went. One has only to go to meetings of Alcoholics Anonymous to find plenty of people whose alcoholism was far
worse than mine; yet they have been without drink for many
years. I am convinced that in the overwhelming majority of
cases alcoholism is a disease and is curable in every sense
other than that an alcoholic cannot become an ordinary
social drinker. The first and essential step, without which no
progress is possible, is for the alcoholic to realise that he is an
alcoholic. I believe that the best way to achieve this is to
accept the test which I accepted when I first came to realise
to some extent the truth about myself. *Anyone who has brought
serious trouble on himself or his family due to drinking and who then
continues to drink must be an alcoholic whether the definitions and
the theories say so or not.* The game has so obviously ceased to
be worth the candle that the player must be mentally un-
balanced to continue. Where there is a complete dis-
proportion between the pleasure obtained by drinking and
the consequences to the drinker in pocket, in health, in self-
respect, and above all in his relationship to other people
and in his work, the drinker is suffering from alcoholism.

It is an intensely difficult subject because, although the
ordinary drinker drinks for pleasure and the alcoholic from

a sort of compulsion, drink satisfies some deep need in man. Wherever man is found in space or time he is almost always accompanied by alcohol. In the dissimilar jungles of Mayfair and Borneo his concern about drink is the same. It must be more than a casual habit, more than an enjoyable custom practised in polite society and abused by the vulgar. On the contrary, heavy drinking has been common among the social aristocracy amd commoner among the real aristocracy of genius. The British Empire was largely founded by hard-drinking adventurers. The three men of genius whom I have known, although of course not alcoholics, are the opposite of teetotallers—Churchill, Augustus John and Aneurin Bevan. Their way of life, of which alcohol is a part, gives rise to their real strength. They do not rely on official files for their information. Over drinks they get to know men in a way which would have been utterly impossible for an austere, almost unapproachable teetotaller like Sir Stafford Cripps. They also discover facts or find the means to discover facts in ways which would not be open to less generous and open natures. They do not reap these rewards deliberately. They are the gift of Bacchus to those who can drink wine graciously and with a genuine liking for their fellow-men. Moreover, if we think of the man of genius of modern times who loathed alcohol, we think of the most evil man of the age, Adolf Hitler. So it is terribly important that the lessons of alcoholism should be limited to true alcoholism.

The outward and visible signs by which an ordinary drinker can be distinguished from an alcoholic are not in dispute. The most important are food, work and exercise. Alcohol is a 'fuel food', liberating energy for the immediate needs of the body, but not leaving a reserve for future use. This I first learned at a meeting of the Parliamentary and Scientific Committee, at which distinguished experts on alcoholism were present, when I managed to steer the conversation round to the subject. (Possibly of course I flatter myself, and a well-meaning friend was responsible.) The consensus of opinion was that people who die of alcoholism die of starvation. They wither away through lack of the real food which they have ceased to eat through loss of appetite. But a man may become an alcoholic even if he continues to eat. I did. So although it is true that a man who eats well, works hard and takes exercise is most unlikely to be an alcoholic, however much he drinks, the matter is not so simple as that.

Churchill is a perfect example of the very opposite of an alcoholic in spite of his phenomenal capacity for drink. I have never seen him, even in his garden at Chartwell or when bricklaying near his home, without a drink ready to hand. Once I lunched alone with him, and before I left at four o'clock we had consumed a bottle (or 'pint' as he calls it) and a half of champagne, two glasses of port and nearly a whole bottle of brandy. It had not the slightest effect on him. Although then a hardened drinker, I was only just about able to function in the evening after a hot bath and a sleep. By then he would already have been at work with a whisky and soda at his side. But of course he does not drink quickly and there is a great deal of soda in the whisky. He never gets drunk even at the end of a very long and tiring day. His mind is always alert and masterful.

He is a good, regular eater. He is a prodigious worker. He loves to take exercise, walking in his garden to admire his beloved animals, ranging from butterflies to goldfish, or even working as a bricklayer. In all this he is a classic example of the ordinary social drinker as against the alcoholic.

Judged by the tests which I suggest distinguish the alcoholic from the normal drinker, Churchill is the very opposite of the alcoholic. Although a man of immense energy, he has no nervous tension to release. He has himself written that all his life, including during the Battle of Britain, he had only to put his head on the pillow to fall into a peaceful sleep almost at once. Probably the secret is that he exhausts his nervous energy by hard work. Certainly his capacity for work and the strict standards of work that he sets himself and others are as unusual as is his genius.

That he has never suffered from a guilt complex or been an escapist is obvious. He has always had a happy home life.

It may be asked: 'Why then does he wish to use alcohol?' No doubt the answer is that he drinks for the same reason as other social drinkers—for the pleasure of the relaxation which it gives. Over a glass of wine Churchill can be the youngest as well as the wisest member of the party. I shall never forget how in one of those magic moments when he allows his mind to ramble delightfully aloud, he said to me —I was then a Labour member—'In the days of my youth I would say with pride, "My father was Chancellor of the Exchequer, my grandfather held high office in the State, my great-great-grandfather was the famous Duke of Marlborough who won the battles of Malplaquet, Oudenarde, Ramillies and Blenheim. I was educated at Harrow. I fought at Omderman—the last time the British formed a square. I have struck with my sabre and fired my pistol for the honour and glory of the British Commonwealth and Empire." But to say this, Raymond, with our Socialist administrators in power, would be highly unfashionable. Today to be in the pink, one must say, "I was born in the workhouse, educated at Borstal. No one has the slightest idea who my father was. My mother died drunk in a brothel." '

While I should still prefer Churchill drunk to any other politician sober, I do not believe that anyone has ever seen him drunk.

There can be no doubt that other people besides Churchill drink enormous quantities without becoming alcoholics. A friend of mine who is well known in Fleet Street is an expert on food and drink. Recently he was charged for the first time in thirty-six years driving with being under the influence of drink. He wisely elected to go for trial before a jury. When he went into the witness-box, the following cross-examination by prosecuting counsel took place:

COUNSEL: Is it true that you admitted to the police surgeon that, apart from your share of a bottle of claret at lunch and some port, you had consumed twenty-four large whiskies during the day?

X: It is.

COUNSEL: And I suppose you now wish us to believe that you had had nothing like so much?

X: On the contrary. On reflection I think I may have had more.   (*Sensation in court.*)

COUNSEL: How on earth can you say that after taking such
an enormous quantity of drink you were not
drunk?

X: Because I am a professional drinker.

COUNSEL (deflated): What do you mean by that?

X: I make my living by being a connoisseur of wines
and of food.

Later the judge had the generosity to say, 'Whatever
view you take of this case, you may doubt whether a franker
defendant has ever been in the witness box.' But my friend
scored heavily by having taken far more pains over the
detailed evidence concerning the road than anyone else,
including the police. (This of course no alcoholic would have
done.) He was acquitted. The judge's only comment was,
'Mr X., it is now twenty-six minutes past two.' The local
closing time was two-thirty. This was one of those unfortunately increasingly rare cases which make a man proud
to be British.

Even so, this man, like Churchill, is altogether exceptional.
They both have constitutions which enable them to do something which few other men could do. Although physically
dissimilar, they are fundamentally alike—adventurous, with
a boyish sense of fun, genuinely anxious to see the good in
others. My friend even went up to the hunchback civilian
who had started his prosecution to shake hands after the case
was over. Churchill has an obsession to be friends with the
Germans. I was with him on his seventy-fifth birthday. What
pleased him most were the telegrams he received from all
the German provincial Prime Ministers. I believe that on
the subject of Germany, and on this alone, Churchill is
below his normal level in realism. But one must admire his
character for it. There is a little-known text in St John: 'If
a man love not his brother whom he can see, how shall he
love God whom he cannot see?' Whether they love God or
not, these men love their fellow-men and it is part of the
expression of that love that they enjoy good company and
the wine that so often goes with it.

Most ordinary people feel the same way—just how deeply
I discovered in a somewhat peculiar fashion. I went into a

hospital to try to complete my self-cure with medical help. An old antique dealer was brought into the bed opposite me by his son and daughter-in-law. They evidently disapproved of his conduct and believed that he was to blame for having been drinking too heavily. He was classified as an alcoholic. Although most depressed he surprised everyone by producing from his fertile brain much Cockney wit and humour. The rest of us alcoholics in the ward began to doubt whether he was really one of us, when he told us that the most he had been drinking was about four large whiskies per day. However, his family believed that he was an alcoholic; he was down in the books as an alcoholic and for his part he did not seem to care what label he was given, or even very much what happened to him.

Four days later I was told the sad news that the old man had been diagnosed as a diabetic—and quite a serious case of diabetes at that. This of course explained why he had been so depressed, why he had fallen off a bus, and why on a relatively small consumption of drink he had been classified as an alcoholic. When I returned to the ward he was sitting with two friends of his who had visited him. He looked as pleased as Punch (to whom by an odd chance he bore some facial resemblance). 'Thank God I now know what's wrong', he said. 'I knew I wasn't an alcoholic. It's only diabetes. Why, I can drink again.' 'Yes', said one of his friends. 'Life would not be worth living without a drink. What a lucky man you are!'

The subject cannot, however, be airily dismissed by saying that one man's drink is another man's poison. Far too much damage is done by excessive drinking and by alcoholism, not only to those who drink, but—which is immeasurably worse—to their families and even to third parties. The liquor advertisements quote Falstaff: 'Good faith, this same young sober-blooded boy doth not love me, nor a man cannot make him laugh; but that's no marvel— he drinks no wine.' They do not give the other side of the picture from Othello: 'O God, that men should put an enemy in their mouths to steal away their brains! That we should with joy, pleasaunce, revel and applause, transform ourselves into beasts.' There is a tradition that Shakespeare himself died of a fever caught after a merry meeting with Ben Jonson.

My object is to point out that there are people whom we call alcoholics, who cannot make drink their servant; to show how they behave; to explain the difference between them and the heavy drinker or ordinary social drinker; and above all, to attempt to do what has not yet been done, to give a clue to enable a drinker or his friends to know that he is a potential alcoholic before he has learned it the hard way. Certainly every heavy drinker should ask himself whether he is in process of becoming an alcoholic.

CHAPTER XVIII

The Reasons

THERE is a Scottish story of a Calvinist minister who preached on the torments of the damned in hell and their protestations that they would not have been such sinners if they had known what Hell would be like. 'And the Lord God Almighty looked down from Heaven in his infinite mercy and said, "Well, ye ken the noo." ' In a way the experts are rather like this version of the Almighty. The doctors say that from a medical or physiological point of view it is impossible to tell the alcoholic from the heavy drinker. Alcoholics Anonymous define an alcoholic as 'any person whose indulgence in alcohol continuously or periodically results in behaviour such as to disrupt normal relations in his or her work, family or society, and is of such a nature as to cause trouble'. In practice this means that a man cannot be told that he is an alcoholic until he has brought very serious trouble, if not ruin, on himself or his family.

Arthur James Balfour once said, 'This is a singularly ill-contrived world, but not as ill-contrived as that.' If alcoholism is a disease—and I am sure from my own experience and the experiences of others that it is itself a disease and not merely a symptom—there must be some physiological difference between the alcoholic and the ordinary drinker. But in the meantime, before this difference is discovered, there must be some pointer to help diagnose the alcoholic before he has got into serious trouble. The first essential step is to convince a man that he is a potential alcoholic. To do that one needs to be able to show him the difference between his drinking and that of the ordinary drinker. I believe that I have found an important clue which has so far been applicable to the alcoholics I have met, in or out of hospital.

The idea that there must be some such clue arose in my mind because there was one man and one man only who warned me that I was an alcoholic long before anyone else, and indeed at a time when nobody would have thought that I was more than an intermittently heavy drinker. That man was David Kirkwood, then Clydeside M.P., a tremendous fighter for the workers yet a friend of Sir Winston Churchill. It was in 1946 that Kirkwood stopped me in the lobby of the House of Commons and said: 'Blackburn, there is something I badly want to say to you, and I hope you will not take it amiss. You must give up the drink. I saw my father kill himself with whisky, and I would never let a chance go by to save someone else from a similar fate. Don't ask me how I know, because I cannot tell you. But I am certain that you are an alcoholic and an alcoholic cannot control his drinking. He has to give it up completely.' I thanked him for trying to help me and immediately went downstairs to the Strangers' Bar and told a friend of mine about it. We laughed our heads off. We kept on coming back to the same joke as the evening wore on with round after round of drinks—and all the time I was proving Kirkwood right without knowing it.

I have often wondered what it was in me that made Kirkwood talk to me like that. Evidently it was something I had in common with his father. Gulping drinks? As a matter of fact I may have gulped the first drink in the morning—when nobody was looking—from time to time, but I certainly drank no more quickly than anyone else. I have asked myself whether it was the Jekyll-Hyde characteristic by which an alcoholic has an entirely different character when drunk from his sober self. But that applies to people other than alcoholics. Moreover, I had never been with Kirkwood, when drunk. The more I thought about Kirkwood's extraordinary insight into my real self, the more convinced I became that it had to do with something deeper than the outward signs of a disease; that, although he could not find the words to explain the basis of his diagnosis, he knew that the very nature of my drinking was different from that of other people; in short, that I drank for a different reason from the normal drinker.

I am convinced that alcoholics are people who drink not for pleasure but to satisfy some deep-seated need or purpose. The normal man drinks for good companionship, for the sense of well-being which drink gives and because it is an accepted practice in certain kinds of society. He does not feel the need for drink, but drinks because he enjoys it.

'If all be true that I do think,
There are five reasons we should drink.
Good wine—a friend—or being dry,
Or lest we should be by and by,
Or any other reason why.'

Perhaps the best reason of all is that drink has a wonderful facility for bringing colour and romance into a world that at times seems dull and shabby. That is why what the vintners sell is so precious.

The alcoholic, however, does not drink primarily for pleasure. Of course, he may have started drinking for the same reasons as anyone else, but by the time he has become an alcoholic or potential alcoholic he no longer drinks only for pleasure. The great thing is that if they were asked why they drank, most of them would realise the truth. The alcoholic drinks for one of two main reasons: either to relieve nervous tension or to ease a guilt complex. Two subsidiary reasons for alcoholic drinking are escapism and to induce sleep. I have yet to meet an alcoholic who does not acknowledge that the fundamental reason for his excessive drinking was to relieve nervous tension, to ease a guilt complex, or escapism. In most cases all three played their part in the end, although the most common original cause (except perhaps with Irishmen) was nervous tension.

If this theory is correct, it should enable a friend or relative of a drinker who is suspected of becoming an alcoholic to induce him to see his danger before it is too late. Of course, in the very early stages of drinking everyone drinks for the same reason—because it is the thing to do, because it is an adventure. But the nature of a man's drinking very soon becomes clear. By the time he has formed drinking habits, he should know the real reason for his drinking. One pointer, which is very often significant, concerns

H

his attitude towards getting drunk. The normal drinker does not like to lose control of himself. He experiences mental and sometimes physical nausea. The alcoholic generally has the opposite reaction. He feels a wild delight that in the mood of abandon induced by drink he can do and say things which would 'make a solicitor's clerk run mad'.

Of course, even if my theory be correct it can at best only help in a few cases. Alcoholics have to find out for themselves that they are suffering from a disease. As by the nature of their disease they lack insight into their own condition, the difficulty of getting them to realise the truth about themselves is very great. The direct approach of telling them that they are alcoholics is generally not only useless but harmful. But if a book is left somewhere for them to read and they pick it up and become interested in it, they may start on the road to possible recovery.

I am sure that alcoholics are the ideal people for helping other alcoholics. At meetings of A.A., where everyone uses his Christian name and it is forbidden to use surnames, there is an extraordinary atmosphere of brotherhood. Some are wealthy and some are poor. Some are happy and others miserable. Some have not drunk for five years, others have 'slipped' often. All recognise that they are alcoholics and that their lives have become unmanageable. Most of them at some time reached rock bottom—divorce, bankruptcy, prison or mental hospital—in my case all four. Many, having with the help of the A.A. given up drink, have restored themselves to their former position and even done better than before (when presumably they were on the way to becoming alcoholics). This is a great encouragement to those who have fallen by the wayside and feel that there is little or no hope for themselves. They see the visible evidence that this terrible disease can be conquered.

The contrast between the members of A.A. is sometimes astonishing. At the first meeting I attended, the man on my right—a man well-known to the other members of the group —was in the depths of despair. We met in a well-known London hotel-cum-public-house where several of us had often had prolonged drinking sessions. The man said: 'Downstairs there are a lot of people forgetting the misery of their lives in drink. I have kept off it for six months and I cannot see what good has come of it. Things are even worse for me now than they have ever been before. I am in dead trouble of all kinds. I would be better off getting drunk downstairs instead of listening to you lot talking about the need for getting rid of self-pity and resentment. If I am suffering from such things, I would get rid of them better with a bottle of gin.' But he did not go and he did not drink. He heard a man say a few minutes later: 'Our friend has not yet reached rock bottom or he would not have spoken like that. I did three years ago. Now I thank God every night that I have had such a wonderful day and been able, by giving up drink, to get back to my job and rebuild my broken life. Today I have had a letter from my sister who had despised and hated me for ten years. No amount of drink could give anyone such joy as that has given me.' He looked, and evidently was, radiantly happy. Between the two extremes of these cases lies the hope of human triumph against disaster and despair. We all knew that the second speaker had been the same as the first speaker three years before and that it was as possible for the one to make a full recovery as it had been for the other.

But the self-cure of an alcoholic is no easy thing. On the contrary it is fiendishly, almost impossibly, difficult. In Spain I met the chief psychiatrist of a Danish hospital, an associate of the men who discovered the drug antabuse. He said publicly that the worst kind of alcoholic—the sort that descends to drinking methylated spirits—is quite incurable and should in the interests of his family and society be given facilities to drink himself to death as quickly as possible. This is a terribly cynical view, but I know that he holds it sincerely. He also believes—as do many others—that alcoholism is not a disease but a symptom of other disorders. I doubt whether this is true. But the intense difficulty of curing a man of alcoholism arises because the fundamental causes which drove him to alcoholism remain and have probably been worsened by his long indulgence in drink. If at first he was suffering from an excess of nervous energy or from a guilt complex or from escapism, or from all three, he is now deeper in trouble than ever before. But he has one supreme ally—the instinct of self-preservation. At some stage of his disastrous journey he has been brought face to face with death and the cold of eternity. He may have murmured to himself:

'Now am I dry of life and death my friend,
There is no ill his magic may not end.'

But faced with the actual prospect of a slow, disgraceful death, he has recoiled in horror. So long as that memory remains upon him, he must fight with the courage of despair. The immediate danger is not great, but sooner or later, when he feels that he is safe, the danger returns worse than ever before. Once an alcoholic always an alcoholic. He can never again drink normally like other people.

Generally the alcoholic must cure himself of the selfish and lazy habits into which he has fallen in the course of his drinking. He must fill the emptiness of his life with hard work and with unselfish deeds. That is why A.A. is so useful. It gives a man back his self-respect by enabling him to help others suffering from the same disease. The rules of A.A.— the twelve steps, as they are called—sound like canons of a religious body. However, the most that the majority of A.A. members claim is that they have accepted Step One—'We admitted we were powerless over alcohol—that our lives had become unmanageable.' Other steps betray the influence of the Oxford Group and would be impossible of fulfilment in most cases, even if a man were a cat and had nine lives. Step 6: 'Were entirely ready to have God remove all these defects of character.' Step 8: 'Made a list of all persons we had harmed and became willing to make amends to them all.' Step 9: 'Made direct amends to such people wherever possible, except when to do so would injure them or others.' When I have suggested at A.A. meetings that this is too much to ask of a man who is only just managing to pull himself out of the jaws of disaster, I have been told that a man can only be expected to achieve what is possible for him. I even heard an American say, 'When people reproach me with what I did during my drunk days, I only say, "I was a sick man".'

Although the religious element is not unduly stressed in A.A., it is regarded as a factor of supreme importance. The connection between religion and alcohol—let alone alcoholism—is undeniable, but so far as I am aware has not been the subject of a scholarly work.

Alcohol is used and has been used in many religions either as the means for or as the symbol of the release of the soul from the fetters of the body. The worshippers of the Greek god Dionysus—the equivalent of the Roman Bacchus—believed that through drink the soul can reach a state of ecstasy and of communion with God or with a god. Oddly enough there is a strange phenomenon known as an 'anaesthetic revelation', and, although no more than an agnostic who would like to believe in the Christian religion, I have experienced a similar alcoholic revelation. My father had a like experience under gas. Mine occurred during an all-night sitting in the smoking room of the House of Commons where I had been drinking fairly heavily. By some extraordinary telepathy the fact that I was undergoing this experience was communicated to my next-door neighbour in the armchair on my right-hand side. It only lasted a few seconds but to me it seemed to be an eternity.

It has been described by Dostoievsky, who enjoyed the same experience immediately before an epileptic fit. There is a feeling of supreme peace. The problems which torture us, including the problems of pain and of evil and of our own sin, are by-passed and vanish in the light and warmth of an all-pervading love which is somehow neither vague nor sentimental, but realistic, adventurous and full of tolerant humour. God is more a Brother than a Father. I remember a distinct feeling of surprise that so many millions of human beings (myself included) should live in such ignorance of the strange and infinite range of God's love. In one respect only was my experience different from that of Dostoievsky. He said that the joy was so great that he knew he could not endure it for more than a few seconds without burning himself out and being destroyed. In the alcoholic revelation there is no such sense that the last few grains of the sands of time are running out. There is relaxation and the assurance

that the happiness and peace is beyond the reach of time.
It is the voice which asks:
'Will ye not come home, brother, home to us again?
We know ye have not wilted in the wind and the rain.
We know that ye have suffered a century of pain,
So will ye not come home, brother, home to us again,
And learn by the fireside, a truth that I'll vow,
That time is past and future, but eternity is now?'
From the medical point of view alcohol frees the lower
nervous centres from the control of the higher. But present-
day medical knowledge on the functioning of the human mind
is very limited, as indeed is clear from the fact that there is
no medical test by which the alcoholic can be distinguished
from the ordinary drinker. The study of mental diseases and
of mental abnormalities is not only perplexing but even
dangerous. One should perhaps be surprised that so few
rather than so many psychiatrists are themselves touched
by the diseases which they study. Certainly there is no
rational or medical ground on which a reasonable person
could assert that experiences of the kind that I have described
are utterly worthless. It cannot be coincidence that the
worshippers of Dionysus, the Indo-Aryan tribes of India, the
North American Indian, the Aztecs and the Incas all
believed that as a result of drink the soul can be released from
the fetters of the body and have some communion with the
mysterious power which supports the universe. To put it
shortly, it may be that the inhibitions which alcohol releases,
separates man from the divine.

We in the West live in an age of lack of faith, and as a
result there is widespread misery and neurosis. There are
only three supremely happy faces I have seen recently. They
were the faces of two nuns and a monk who were obviously
where 'beyond those voices there is peace'. While awaiting
trial I read many accounts of the torture and death of men
and women for their religious principles in the Middle Ages.
The astonishing fact is the happiness which shines through
the words they utter on the scaffold. Occasionally, as with
Vanzetti's 'That agony is our triumph', we hear an echo
of the same note even today. But in general the accent is on

material welfare, on cars and television sets and washing-
machines. The body becomes more comfortable and the soul
more uneasy. It is most significant that the experience of
Alcoholics Anonymous proves that alcoholics cannot generally
cure themselves with a belief in some power greater than
themselves.

As for me, the issue remains undecided at the time of
writing. In an alcoholic bout, I wrote—I only write my
so-called poetry in such bouts—as an epitaph for a friend:

> When the wine is finished,
> And love is dead,
> And the long fight's over,
> May this be said:
> 'Though God he loved not,
> Or would not see,
> Yet he loved his brother
> Whom he could see.'

But in my sober moments I do not believe that humanism
can be a substitute for religion. The mystery of our origin
and the search for our long home are deeply embedded in
the human heart. We can only pray for more light.

No man has the right to expect his own private revelation
of eternal truth—if indeed the word 'truth' is not qualified by
relativity. There can be no excuse for a man to continue in
his path to alcoholic self-destruction because he cannot see
God. He must cure himself or acknowledge that he is no man.

Complete abstinence is at first a wonderful experience for
the alcoholic. His health is restored. He sleeps soundly.
He feels the strength and the love of life pouring back into
his veins. He can delight again in simple things. But then
he finds that the clock has gone back to his youth—and
generally he is no longer young. (Most alcoholics are in a
sense Peter Pans.) He resumes the hopes and fears, the
passions and the torments of his youth. He is a man born
again, but he faces a harsh world in which he has lately cut
a sorry figure. There must be, there *is* a cure.

Antabuse, the drug discovered in Denmark, can be a
great help. If a man takes an antabuse pill he knows that he
cannot drink for twenty-four hours without being terribly

ill. I once drank a few glasses of wine about twelve hours after taking antabuse. At first I became flushed. My heart appeared to be pumping against an overwhelming tide of resistance. Finally I felt such nausea that I wished myself dead. I certainly never wanted to go through such an experience again.

Antabuse is a wonderful temporary expedient—but it is no cure. The cure lies deeper.

The cure lies in regular work, food and habits, in a good home and, above all, someone to live for. The love of another may save even the alcoholic who cannot believe in God.

When I was at my worst, someone believed that I was inhabited by the Devil. To psychologists this would be an idle belief, a myth acceptable only to the ignorant and the primitive. I am persuaded that it is not without its share of the truth and is indeed nearer reality than the theories of Freud and his successors. Above all it has a strange purity and cleanliness. It can enable a man to accept his own guilt without blaming it on his forefathers or his upbringing. It can help him feel that here in our transitory lives we are soldiers in a supreme battle in which something of permanent value may be attained. It can restore dignity to a world whose face becomes even more shallow as man's material achievements grow greater. The scientists may find the evidence of their theories in the twilight of the mind. This theory of the eternal conflict between good and evil, between God and the Devil, is as old as man and more profound than their wisdom. It brings the hope of forgiveness to the guilty. To those who thirst for beauty, it brings its image and its comfort. It can make a man welcome the rolling tides of time and fight once again the lost battle of his honour. Whether he succeeds or fails, for a moment or for eternity he has breathed the very breath of life and felt the mysterious joy of that unseen world which surely lies within us.